South American Props

GW00584966

RON MAK

HISTORIC COMMERCIAL AIRCRAFT SERIES, VOLUME 15

Title page: A cargo truck and a C-46 at Bogotá El Dorado Airport, Colombia, on February 22, 1993.

Contents page: The Air Colombia maintenance area at Bogotá El Dorado Airport.

Back cover: A Bolivian B-17 at La Paz El Alto Airport, Bolivia.

Front cover: Two C-46s at Bogotá El Dorado Airport on February 22, 1993.

Published by Key Books
An imprint of Key Publishing Ltd
PO Box 100
Stamford
Lincs PE9 1XQ

www.keypublishing.com

The right of Ron Mak to be identified as the author of
this book has been asserted in accordance with
the Copyright, Designs and Patents Act 1988
Sections 77 and 78.

Copyright © Ron Mak, 2023

ISBN 978 1 80282 573 2

All rights reserved. Reproduction in whole or in part
in any form whatsoever or by any means is strictly
prohibited without the prior permission of the Publisher.

Typeset by SJmagic DESIGN SERVICES, India.

Contents

Introduction...4

Chapter 1 Venezuela 5

Chapter 2 Suriname...18

Chapter 3 Brazil..20

Chapter 4 Paraguay..29

Chapter 5 Uruguay 31

Chapter 6 Argentina...32

Chapter 7 Chile..41

Chapter 8 Bolivia..47

Chapter 9 Peru..61

Chapter 10 Ecuador..70

Chapter 11 Colombia...75

Introduction

This book has come about from my travels to South America between 1971 and 1993. I visited many airports in Venezuela, Suriname, Brazil, Paraguay, Uruguay, Argentina, Chile, Bolivia, Peru, Ecuador, and Colombia during those years, taking pictures of small airliners, helicopters, cargo and passenger, and civilian and military aircraft. I traveled through most of the larger airports in those countries, photographing as many prop planes as I could. I hope you enjoy them!

Ron Mak
Almere, The Netherlands
February 22, 2023

Trans Aereos Illimani Curtis C-46A at La Paz El Alto Airport, undergoing engine maintenance.

Chapter 1

Venezuela

AVENSA Curtiss C-46A YV-C-AVK at Caracas Maiquetía Airport, Venezuela, in November 1972. Delivered to the United States Army Air Force (USAAF) as 41-12338 (msn 26465) on April 17, 1943, it transferred to the Reconstruction Finance Corporation (RFC) on November 6, 1945, and was later stored at Walnut Ridge Air Force Station in Arkansas in June 1949 as N5807V. It was bought by AVENSA in July 1955, registered as YV-C-AVK on July 11, 1955, and then sold to Latin Carga in 1973 as YV-C-TGH. The aircraft was reregistered as YV-140C in 1975, and written off on August 1, 1977, near Maiquetía; the cause of the accident is unknown. (R. M. Collection)

Aeropostal YV-04C HS 748-215 at Caracas Maiquetía Airport on October 20, 1977. Delivered to Linea Aeropostal Venezolana as YV-C-AME (msn 1577) on May 15, 1965, it was reregistered in November 1975 as YV-04C. It was bought by RegionAir (which merged with Quebecair in March 1984) in January 1982 as C-GDUI, then sold to Bradley Air Services on September 25, 1987. The registration was cancelled in September 1990 and the aircraft was broken up at Carp Airport, Ontario, in March 1991.

AVENSA Convair CV580 YV-63C at Mérida Alberto Carnevalli Airport, Venezuela, on October 22, 1977. This aircraft was ordered by Varig as PP-AQF (msn 446) but was not taken up, it was instead bought by AVENSA as YV-C-EVJ in July 1957 and converted from a CV-440 to a CV-580 in June 1969. It was reregistered as YV-63C in 1976 and sold to Plymouth Leasing as N4862M in November 1979. On January 26, 1981, it was reregistered as N589PL for lease to Air New England, and returned in November of that year. It was subsequently leased to Sierra Pacific until September 1983; bought by Prinair in October 1983; sold to Executive Car & Truck Leasing Inc on May 31, 1985, and stored at Gainsville, Florida; bought by Kelowna Flightcraft Air Charter as C-GKFP in March 1990; and then sold to Nolinor Aviation in November 2005. On August 3, 2011, the aircraft's nose gear collapsed upon landing at Kasba Lake Airport, Northwest Territories, Canada, and it was damaged beyond repair.

Aero B Douglas DC-6A/B YV-290C at Caracas Maiquetía Airport on October 14, 1979. Delivered to Pan American World Airways as *Clipper Balbao* (msn 44107) on September 30, 1953, it was converted from a DC-6B to a DC-6A/B in 1960. It was sold to the Portuguese Air Force (Força Aérea Portuguesa) as 6701 on June 26, 1961, and after 17 years of service it was bought by Atlas Aircraft Corporation as N789TA in September 1978. Sold to Aero B Venezuela on November 12, 1978 as YV-290C *Caracas*, it was bought by an unknown operator as YV-2343P in the mid 1980s and then sold to Transporte Aero Dominicano (TRADO) in October 1985 as HI-454CT. It was withdrawn from use (wfu) and stored at Santo Domingo Airport in the Dominican Republic in July 1991.

Orinoco Mining Company Fairchild F-27A YV-O-CFO-1 at Ciudad Guayana Airport, Puerto Ordaz, on October 20, 1979. Delivered to the United States Steel Corporation on November 19, 1959, as N12500 (c/n 67), it was converted from an F-27A to an F-27F in August 1961. Subsequently bought by the Orinoco Mining Company on December 22, 1967 as YV-P-APZ, it was then sold to the Corporacion Ferrominera del Orinoco as YV-O-CFO-1. In November 1981, it was bought by the Miami Aviation Corporation as N108AS and leased to Air Pacific Airlines in July 1982, being bought by the latter on August 31, 1983. It was sold to Seattle Aviation Inc in March 1987 and bought by the General Aviation Service in May 1989, later being wfu and scrapped at an unknown location.

RUTACA Convair CV-440-48 YV-223C at Ciudad Bolivar Tomás de Heres Airport (more commonly known as Ciudad Bolivar Airport), Venezuela, on October 21, 1979. Delivered to KLM Royal Dutch Airlines on January 18, 1954, as a Convair 340-48 with the registration PJ-CVS *Saba* (c/n 144), it was reregistered as PH-CGC on August 27, 1954, and renamed *Jacob Maris*. It was converted to CV-440 standard and reregistered as PJ-CVC on May 15, 1963, then transferred to ALM Antillean Airlines as *Corsow* on August 1, 1964. In February 1970, the aircraft was bought by Aviation Business Service as N12171, then subsequently sold to East Coast Aviation in October 1972, and later AVENSA as YV-C-AVT in 1973, although the company later reregistered it as YV-58C in August 1975. RUTACA purchased the aircraft as YV-223C in 1977, then sold it to Tecnofly in 1986; it was then bought by Aeroejecutivos in 1999 as YV-223C, with which it was then stored and wfu at Caracas Maiquetía Airport in March 2003.

Aeropostal DHC-6-300 Twin Otter YV-29C at Ciudad Bolivar Airport on October 21, 1979. Delivered to Linea Aeropostal Venezuela S.A. (LAV) on April 19, 1977, as YV-29C (c/n 524), the aircraft was bought by Linea Turistica Aerotuy (LTA) as YV-529C in January 1988 and sold to World Jet Aircraft Sales and Leasing in June 1993 as N81708. With this company, it was leased to Seaborne Airlines as N251SA from June 1996 until February 2003, then reregistered to Plane Llc Salem in Oregon and stored in January 2015, before being bought by Aero Ruto Maya S.A. on June 29, 2016, as TG-JCA. It was still operational in Guatemala during 2022.

Transporte Transilaca Sud Aviation SA-316B Alouette III YV-243CP at Canaima airstrip, in the southeast of Venezuela, on October 20, 1979. The Sud Aviation 316B Alouette was built in France and made its first flight in 1959, proving popular with operators around the world due to the type's strong high-altitude characteristics. Transporte Transilaca had two Alouettes, YV-243CP and YV-244CP, which were both based at Canaima and used for ambulance flights for tourists who get into trouble whilst visiting the Canaima National Park, home to the famous Angel Falls waterfall, where the drop is almost 1,000m.

Aeronaves del Centro Short SD-330-200 YV-373C at Valencia Arturo Michelena International Airport, Valencia, on October 31, 1983. Completed by Short Brothers on June 13, 1980, as G-BHWU (c/n SH-3050), it was delivered to Aeronavas del Centro on August 20, 1980, as YV-373C. Aeronvas del Centro was based at Valencia Arturo Michelena International Airport, with two Short 330s (YV-374C and YV-373C) that flew within Venezuela from Valencia to Caracas, Barcelona and Porlamar. The company ceased operations during 1987, and YV-374C was wfu at Caracas Maiquetía Airport, while YV-373C was wfu at Valencia Arturo Michelena.

Corporacion Ferrominera de Orinoco S.A. Consolidated PBY-5As YV-585CP (c/n 1774) and YV-584CP (c/n 1736) at Manuel Carlos Piar Guayana International Airport, both wfu and up for sale, on November 1, 1983. The two Catalinas were used to fly crews to the dredging barges on the Orinoco and Caroni rivers; the Catalinas flew to the barge twice a week to relieve the crews working 24 hours a day to open an important fairway that enabled large ships to navigate the rivers and serve the industry around Ciudad Guayana, especially the steel factories. Eventually, the Catalinas were replaced by two Canadair Cl-215s. YV-584CP remained wfu at Manuel Carlos Piar Guayana, but YV-585CP was restored to flying condition and flew to Maiquetía with its new owner, Serves, in 1993. Sadly, YV-585CP was once again wfu, this time at Luis Muñoz Marín International Airport, Puerto Rico, from 2000 until 2004, and then later dismantled and shipped to Australia in 2013. In 2015, it was transferred to the Royal Australian Air Force's (RAAF) Rathmines Catalina base.

Aero B Venezuela Douglas DC-6A/B YV-290C at Caracas Maiquetía Airport on November 3, 1983. Delivered to Pan American World Airways on September 30, 1953, as N6107C *Clipper Balboa* (c/n 44107), it was converted from a DC-6B to a cargo DC-6A/B in 1960 and bought by the Portuguese Air Force with the serial 6701 on June 26, 1961. It was sold to the Atlas Aircraft Corporation as N789TA in September 1978 and bought by Aero B Venezuela on November 12, 1978. Aero B Venezuela was founded in April 1978 by ex-military pilots, and the company initially flew two Convair CV-340s and a Douglas DC-6A on contract work, which included importing flowers from Colombia. Eventually, the two Convair CV-240s were sold, and four Douglas DC-6A/Bs (including YV-290C) were bought to assist the single DC-6A. The company ceased operations during 1984/1985.

Aero B Venezuela Douglas DC-6A/B YV-295C at Caracas Maiquetía Airport on November 3, 1983. This DC-6 does not yet have the color scheme of Aero B Venezuela, instead retaining the livery of Sociedade Acoreana de Transportes Aereos (SATA) from the Azores. Delivered first to Pan American World Airways as N6258C *Clipper Gladiator* (c/n 44258) on May 1, 1954, it was bought by the Portuguese Air Force as 6703 on August 21, 1961. In 1976, the aircraft was sold to SATA as CS-TAN, then to Aero B Venezuela as YV-295C during 1980 and named *Porlamar*. Purchased by Universal Airlines in July 1984 as N400UA, it was then reregistered to Ball Albert Newton on September 2, 1992, and bought by the company in 1995. The aircraft was sold to Everts Air Cargo on May 30, 2003, wfu and parked at Fairbanks International Airport graveyard for spare part donation in 2010.

Ministry of Transport and Communications (Ministerio de Transportes y Comunicaciones) YV-O-MTC12 at Maiquetía Simón Bolívar International Airport on November 3, 1983. Delivered to the USAAF as 41-7747 (c/n 4234), this aircraft became NC52709 and was bought by the Ministry of Transport and Communications in 1949 as YV-O-MC3. It had several registrations, including YV-MC1, YV-O-MC2, YV-O-MT2 and YV-O-MC1, and was wfu in November 1983.

Latin Carga Curtiss C-46A YV-143C at Caracas Maiquetía Airport on November 3, 1983. Delivered to the USAAF as 43-47316 (c/n 387) on April 23, 1945, it was sent to the China National Aviation Corporation as XT-120 on May 6, 1945, as part of the lend-lease scheme. It was sold to Westair Transport as N4894V in 1955, then bought by Lineas Aereas Unidas S.A. on November 4, 1957, as XA-MER. Subsequently reregistered as N4894V, the aircraft was exported to Venezuela on September 3, 1963, becoming YV-C-LBR for Linea Expresa Bolivar C.A. on October 15. Transportes Aereos de Carga S.A. bought the aircraft on May 23, 1968 as YV-C-TGD, and Latin Carga reregistered it as YV-143C in 1975. It was wfu at Maiquetía in 1977.

Privately owned de Havilland D.H.114 YV-284P *Heron* at Caracas Maiquetía Airport on November 3, 1983. Delivered to Shell Venezuela on January 6, 1958, it was sold to the Venezuelan Ministry of Mines as YV-P-AEC (c/n 14131), but was not taken up, leading to the subsequent reregistration as YV-284P in 1974 and storage at Opa-locka Airport in Florida by 1979. By July 7, 1986, Air Rarotonga, based in the Cook Islands of the South Pacific, procured the propliner, reregistered it as ZK-TAJ, then withdrew it in April 1992; it was later broken up in Tasmania.

Corpoven Douglas C-47A YV-32CP at Caracas Maiquetía Airport on November 3, 1983. Built as 42-93252 (c/n 13143) on April 28, 1944, this aircraft was assigned to the US 12th Air Force in Italy on June 8 of the same year. In December 1953, it was bought by the Socony-Vacuum Oil Co. (later Mobil), and on May 20, 1957, it was reregistered as YV-P-BPF for the company's Venezuela division. It was officially transferred to Venezuela in 1965 and reregistered as YV-32CP. It flew to Waco Airport in Texas in October 1978 and was converted by Shafer Modifications Inc to feature Pratt & Whitney PT6A-65AR turboprop engines. Later bought by Airworld as ZS-NKK, the aircraft was damaged beyond repair during take-off at Pretoria Wonderboom Airport in South Africa on August 24, 1998.

Helicopteros del Caribe Sikorsky S-55 YV-356C at Caracas Maiquetía Airport on November 4, 1983. Two Sikorsky S-55s were based on a hill with an overview of the airport. They were mainly used to bring tourist to islands off the coast of Venezuela like Islas los Roques, Isla la Orchila and Isla la Tortuga. Following the first flight of the Sikorsky S-55 in November 1949, Sikorsky produced 1067 S-55 military variants for 30 operators throughout the world. Another 547 were built under license by Westwind in the UK, under the name Whirlwind.

Peter Botomme's Consolidated PBY-5A YV-209CP at Charallave Airport on November 4, 1983. Botomme was the founder of Venezuelan TV station RCTV and Radio Caracas radio station, a senior partner of Venezuelan airline Aerotuy and aviation lover; in addition to the Catalina, he also owned a North American P51 Mustang and a Pits Special aerobatic biplane. PBY-5A YV-209CP (c/n 1808), ex-N5519V, was registered to Peter Botomme in 1978, and then sold to Thaddeus Bruno and Enrico Recchi in the US in August 1985 as N285NJ. On May 21, 1989, during a flight from Turin Airport in Italy, the Catalina aquaplaned during take-off and hit a farm fence at the end of the runway, crashing into the farm courtyard; the pilots sadly lost their lives, but the three passengers survived.

Servivensa Douglas C-47A YV-610C arriving at Canaima Airport on February 15, 1993. Delivered to the USAAF as 42-24032 (c/n 9894) on July 22, 1943, it became NC19997 on September 23, 1946, while working for Air France. It was reregistered as F-BCYS on September 8, 1947, for Etat/Secretariat Générale Aviation Civile et Commerciale, then bought by Air Liban Tripol on September 15, 1947, as LR-AAN. In March 1951, it became OD-AAN for Air Liban, which merged with Middle East Airlines (MEA) on September 1, 1965, to become MEA-Air Liban. Bought by the International Aviation Development Corporation as N219F on December 28, 1965, the aircraft was subsequently leased to Phillips Petroleum, Amoco UAR Oil Co and Pyramid Air Lines. On July 22, 1979, it was wfu and stored at Málaga-Costa del Sol Airport, Spain, in 1985; however, in 1989, it was bought by Midas Air Commuter as YV-505C, and then by Servicios Avensa (Servivensa) in 1990. On February 23, 2001, it was seen without engines and wings at Manuel Carlos Piar Guayana International Airport.

Servivensa Carga Douglas DC-3C YV-609C departing Canaima Airport, February 15, 1993. Delivered to Sabena on January 29, 1947 as OO-AUV, it was leased to Linair Lybia in November 1959, then to Bodensee Flugdienst in 1966. The aircraft was bought by Delta Air Transport in March 1970 (still as OO-AUV) and later sold to Jack Adams Aircraft Sales as N3433U in November 1976; from there, it was bought by Buckeye Air Freight, then Meridian Air Cargo and Eagle Airlines in July 1983, before being reregistered as N222PV in October 1985 for Atoire Air from El Paso, Texas. It was sold to AVENSA in January 1989 as YV-98C and transferred to Servivensa in February 1990 as YV-609C; the aircraft was wfu at Canaima Airport in February 2001.

Servivensa Douglas C-47A YV-610C arriving at Canaima Airport on February 15, 1993. The Canaima National Park was created in June 1962 to protect the group of mountains known as the Tepuyes and other sites of incomparable beauty, such as the aforementioned Angel Falls, the highest waterfall in the world. Tourists can see Angel Falls when flying in a Servivensa C-47A en route to Puerto Ordaz, or in a Cessna 172 from Ciudad Bolivar Airport back to Canaima. However, in the author's opinion, the best way to see the waterfall is with the Jungle Rudy tour; "We took this tour in 1979 from the Netherlands. It was an expedition to Angel Falls, and from a height of 979 meters we were able to enjoy breathtaking views. We also spent time walking though wild and exotic flora with an impressive variety of colors, texture and forms. It took us a total of four days back and forth – a great adventure!"

RUTACA Airlines Douglas C-47A YV-224C at Ciudad Bolivar Airport on February 15, 1993. Delivered to USAAF as 42-100592 (c/n 19055) on August 23, 1946, it was later bought by a unknown owner as NC68221, then sold to the Brazilian Air Force (Força Aérea Brasileira, FAB) as FAB-2056 and subsequently to the Brazil government as PP-ETE. In 1982, Rico Linhas Aereas purchased the aircraft as PT-KXR and then sold it to RUTACA Airlines in 1992. On January 25, 2001, RUTACA flight 225 was flying from Canaima Airport to Porlamar Airport on Isla Margarita via Ciudad Bolivar Airport for a fuel stop; shortly after take-off, engine problems forced the pilot to return to Tomás de Heres, but during the return the pilot lost control of the C-47A and the aircraft crashed into the residential area near the airport. The C-47A struck a large tree and burst into flames; none of the 20 tourists or four crew members survived.

RUTACA Airlines de Havilland DHC-2 Beaver YV-230C at Ciudad Bolivar Airport on February 16, 1993. Delivered to Aerotaxi on October 27, 1959, as HK-1004X (c/n 1336), the aircraft was sold to Aerovias in early 1992 as HK-1004 and then bought by Comeravia as YV-C-CMB in November 1992. At some point, it was reregistered as YV-178C and bought by RUTACA as YV-206C, then reregistered as YV-230C on April 7, 1992. It was exported to Hillfield Leasing Inc in Canada in 1999 as C-FZXD.

Pilot James "Jimmie" Crawford Angel's Flamingo G-2-W NC9487 (serial 11) at Ciudad Bolivar Airport on February 16, 1993. The American pilot and explorer was born on August 1, 1899, in Cedar Valley, Missouri. Until Jimmie Angel flew over them on November 16, 1933, while searching for a valuable ore bed, Angel Falls, which cascades from the top of Auyantepui, was unknown to the outside world. On October 9, 1937, he returned to the falls with the intention of landing; however, despite a successful touchdown, his aircraft, *El Rio Caroni*, nose-dived when it hit soft ground at the end of its landing and the wheels sank in the mud, making take-off impossible. It took him 11 days on foot to reach the nearest settlement at Kamarata. His aircraft remained atop the Auyantepui until 1970, when it was disassembled and brought down by Venezuelan military helicopters. The Flamingo is now displayed at Ciudad Bolivar Airport's main terminal, and Jimmie Angel gave his name to the stunning waterfall. He died on December 8, 1956.

Right: Angel Falls is the world's highest uninterrupted waterfall. It tumbles from a cleft near the summit of table-top mountain Auyán Tepui into what is known as Devil`s Canyon, 3212ft (979m) below. A truly unforgettable spectacle.

Below: RUTACA Airlines Douglas DC-3C YV-218C at Ciudad Bolivar Airport on February 16, 1993. Delivered to Waterman Airlines as NC33695 in 1946 (c/n 43079), it was sold to TACA de Venezuela as YV-C-AZA. The latter company merged with Linea Aeropostal Venezuela S.A. (LAV) in July 1957. The aircraft was wfu at Caracas Maiquetía Airport in 1968; then sold to Aerotechnica S.A. as YV-C-GAF; reregistered to a private owner as YV-108C; sold to RUTACA Airlines in 1992 as YV-218C; and then wfu at Tomás de Heres in 1999.

Aeroejecutivos Douglas DC-3A YV-440C at Maiquetía International Airport on February 17, 1993. Delivered to American Airlines as NC21797 (c/n 2201) on March 4, 1940, it was converted from a Douglas DC-3-277B to a DC-3A on July 1, 1947, and reregistered as N21797. It was bought by Alex Outdoors Club on June 20, 1968, which then sold it on to Sports International Inc on March 31, 1970. On January 31, 1972, it was sold to Texarkana Aircraft Associates Inc, and on July 19, 1973, Provincetown-Boston Airline purchased the aircraft and later registered it as N31PB on November 30, 1973. It was sold to National Express Airlines Inc on March 31, 1986, and bought by Sekman Aviation Corp on May 23, 1986. Sold to Aeroejecutivos on May 4, 1987 as YV-440C, it was withdrawn from use in 2006 and was still wfu at Metropolitano International Airport, Ocumare del Tuy, south of Caracas, as of March 2021.

Chapter 2
Suriname

Surinam Airways de Havilland DHC-6-310 Twin Otter PZ-TCF at Zorg en Hoop Airport, Paramaribo, on April 14, 1982. Delivered on January 11, 1980 as PZ-TCF (c/n 660) for Surinam Airways, it was leased to Saint Lucia Airways in 1983 and bought by Saint Lucia Airways in December 1984 as J6-SLP. It was then sold to Lentz & Co from Chicago as N456RE on September 19, 1987, and then bought by Devon Holding and Leasing Inc on June 4, 1992 as N933LC. The aircraft was reregistered to Pace Aviation Ltd on December 20, 1993, and bought by Sunflower Airlines in December 1994 as DQ-FIE, later transferring to Sun Air in December 2002. It was sold to the Longview Aviation Corporation on July 8, 2019, as C-GVLA.

Surinam Airways de Havilland DHC-6-300 Twin Otter PZ-TCD at Zorg en Hoop Airport on April 14, 1982. This aircraft (c/n 646) undertook its first flight with de Havilland Canada on October 24, 1979. It was then bought by Desert Sand Leasing on November 6, 1979 as N7015A and leased to Surinam Airways as PZ-TCD in November 1979. On January 23, 2006, it was sold to Gum Air as PZ-TB and remains active with this company as of November 2022. The Twin Otters of Surinam Airways are mainly used on the domestic routes within Suriname, flying from Zorg en Hoop Airport to Djoemoe, Ladouanie, Nickerie, Stoelmanseiland, and Wasjabo.

Southern Air Transport Lockheed L-100-30 Hercules N251SF Paramaribo-Zanderij International Airport on April 19, 1982. Delivered to Safair Freighters on April 24, 1975, as ZS-RSH (c/n 4590), this aircraft was bought by Southern Air Transport in March 1982 as N251SF. It was reregistered as N516SJ in July 1987 and reregistered again in March 1988, this time as N903SJ. From September 27, 1993, it was stored at Tucson Airport, Arizona, until September 19, 1997, when Lynden Air Cargo bought the Lockheed L-100-30 as N403LC. It was still active in November 2022.

Carlos Teixeira Pereira Douglas C-47A PT-KUR at Paramaribo-Zanderij International Airport on April 19, 1982. This aircraft was originally delivered to the USAAF as 42-24070 (c/n 9932), then sold to the Brazilian Air Force (Forca Aerea Brasileira, FAB) as FAB-2044. It was bought by Carlos Teixeira Pereira as PT-KUR and sold to Rondonia Industria y Comercio (RICO Taxi Aereo) on August 7, 1990. It has since been wfu at Manaus International Airport, Brazil.

Chapter 3

Brazil

Varig Douglas C-47A PP-VBF is displayed at Parque do Flamengo, Rio de Janeiro, on November 12, 1973. Delivered to the USAAF on August 30, 1943, it was wfu and stored on January 15, 1946. Soon after, however, on July 19, 1946, it was bought by the Hughes Tool Company as NC68358. It was sold to Varig in December 1947 as PP-VBF and preserved at Parque do Flamengo in September 1971. In January 1980, the C-47A was moved to Rio de Janeiro Galeão Airport after vandals damaged it, and by March of that year it was displayed at the Varig maintenance area. It was scrapped on January 31, 2020, when Varig went bankrupt.

FAB Douglas C-47A FAB-2061 at Galeão Airport in November 11, 1973. In the background, there are two Argentine Navy Lockheed SP-2E Neptunes, 2-P-104 and 105, and a FAB search and rescue (SAR) Grumman HU-16A Albatross with the serial 6538. Delivered to the USAAF as 43-15744 (c/n 20210) in 1943, the C-47A was later bought by the FAB as FAB-2061 and subsequently by Construtora Andrade Gutierrez S.A as PT-KVX. It was sold to RICO Taxi Aerea, then wfu and stored at Manaus International Airport in February 1991.

VASP Douglas DC-6A(C) PP-LFA in Galeão Airport on November 13, 1973. Delivered to Loide Aereo Nacional (LAN) on December 9, 1958, as PP-LFA (c/n 45527), it was leased to Panair do Brasil in 1959 with the name *Fernando de Camargo*. The aircraft was returned to LAN in March 1961, and the company merged with VASP in January 1962. In 1975, it was stored and wfu at São Paulo–Congonhas Airport until it was purchased by Transportes Areos La Cumbre from Bolivia as CP-1283 in July 1977. It was subsequently stored at La Paz El Alto Airport in 1984, and was in poor condition in June 2000; it was derelict in October 2013, still at the airport.

VASP Vickers Viscount V.827 PP-SRC (c/n 397) at Galeão Airport on November 13, 1973. Delivered to VASP on October 28, 1958, this aircraft was bought by PLUNA Uruguay on November 7, 1975. It was sold to Ronald J. Clark in March 1982 as N480RC and stored at Tucson Airport before being bought by Go Transportation in September 1984. It was sold to JadePoint in November 1987 and was scrapped in 1992 at Tucson Airport.

Cruzeiro do Sul, NAMC YS-11A-202 PP-CTI at Rio de Janeiro Santos Dumont Airport on November 10, 1973. It was delivered to Cruzeiro do Sul on October 9, 1968, as PP-CTI (c/n 2080). On April 29, 1977, during a cargo flight to Navegantes International Airport, Itajai, in the province of Santa Catarina, YS-11A made an approach in poor visibility and dense fog, and touched down 460m past the threshold; control was lost and the aircraft sped off the right side of the runway, colliding with light beacons. The nose and left gear collapsed and it was damaged beyond repair; luckily, there were no fatalities.

VASP NAMC YS-11A-212 PP-SMM *Samurai* at Rio de Janeiro Santos Dumont Airport on November 10, 1973. It was delivered to VASP on November 30, 1968, as PP-SMM (c/n 2079). It was then purchased by TOA Domestic Airlines in November 1977 as JA8723 *Kibi*; TOA became Japan Air System on April 1, 1988, and the aircraft was leased to Air Star Zanzibar as JA8723 in March 1994. TCA Ltd bought the aircraft on April 12, 1996, as N995CL and exported it as P4-KFS to KFS Aviation in Aruba in May 1996. It was bought by Air Philippines in November 1996 with the P4-KFS registration, although this was later changed to RP-C1931. The aircraft was then sold to the Air Link Aviation School in 2004 and reregistered as RP-C2252. In May 2019, it was bought by Sakurai Aviation in Sri Lanka and stored at Colombo International Airport, Ratmalana, in October 2021; as of May 2022, it was in the process of being dismantled for a museum in Japan.

FAB Douglas DC-6B FAB-2415 arriving at Galeão Airport on November 11, 1973. Delivered to Western Air Lines as N91302 (c/n 43822) on January 15, 1953, it was bought by Northwest Orient Airlines in 1959 and was later sold to International Air Services (IAS) on August 25, 1961. On the very same day that it was bought by IAS, it was immediately sold on to Varig as PP-YSM, then subsequently, in 1968, to the FAB as 2415. It was sold to the Paraguayan Air Force as T-89 in June 1975 and was re-serialled as 4002 in 1980. In December 1990, it was wfu and stored at Asuncion Airport in Paraguay.

Panair do Brasil Douglas DC-7C PP-PDN *Nicolau Barreto* is wfu and stored at Galeão Airport on November 10, 1973. It was delivered to Panair do Brasil on May 23, 1957, as PP-PDN (c/n 45125) and was wfu and stored at Galeão in February 1968. It was offered for auction on April 28, 1969, but did not sell, and consequently the registration was cancelled in 1971 and the aircraft broken up during 1975.

FAB Fairchild C-82A Packet FAB-2211 at the Brazilian Air Force Aerospace Museum at Afonsos Air Force Base (AFB) on November 10, 1973. Twelve C-82A Packets entered service on September 20, 1955, with the Air Transport Command at Campo dos Afonsos, and they were withdrawn from use on July 9, 1967. The C-82A Packet was a twin-engine, twin-boom cargo and troop aircraft, which had its first flight on September 10, 1944; in total, 223 were built between 1944 and 1948.

FAB Curtiss C-46A FAB-2058 at Afonsos AFB on November 10, 1973. Delivered to the USAAF as 43-47084 (c/n 155) on December 15, 1944, it transferred to the United States Navy on December 16, 1944. It was bought by Vinicius V. Vasconcellos in 1948 as PP-XBR and then transferred to the FAB as FAB-2058. During 1968, it was wfu and stored at Campo dos Afonsos, where it was reregistered as PP-ZBE in 1980 and then sold to Roberto H. Rubaina in 1981 as PT-LBP. After it was sold to Royal Taxi Aereo in 1988, the company refurbished the C-46A and transported it to the Brazilian Air Force Aerospace Museum in FAB livery on July 3, 1998.

FAB PBY-5A Catalina FAB-6509 at Tabatinga air base, in the border area of Brazil, Colombia and Peru, on November 5, 1977. Delivered to the United States Navy as 46456 (c/n 1820) on January 22, 1944, it was sold to the FAB as FAB-10 on December 12, 1944, and reregistered as FAB-6509. Bought by David C. Tallichet of the Project Catalina Inc as N4582T on December 23, 1983, the delivery flight to Fort Lauderdale was in March 1984. In July 1984, the nose gear collapsed upon landing at Springfield Airport, Ohio, and the aircraft was repaired and flown to NAS Pensacola in 1984 for temporary storage. It was subsequently dismantled and transported by truck to Brooklyn, New York, for the Historic Aircraft Restoration Project at the Floyd Bennett Field, where it was assembled and displayed while under restoration between 1997 and 2014.

VOTEC Servicios Aéreos Regionais Fokker F-27-200 PT-LCF at Belem Airport on April 16, 1982. First flown on June 21, 1962 as PH-FDT (c/n 10204) and delivered to Direcção de Exploração de Transportes Aéreos as CR-AIA on July 6, 1962, it was reregistered as C9-AIA in January 1975 and tranferred to Linhas Aéreas de Moçambique in May 1980. In November 1981, it was sold to Manufacturers Hanover Leasing as N379SL and delivered to Votec as PT-LCF in April 1982, which merged with Brasil Central on August 1, 1986. On January 27, 1987, the F-27-200 touched down to the right of the centerline at Varginha Airport during the landing roll; the pilot attempted to control the aircraft, but the right main landing gear collapsed after hitting several runway lights, and the Fokker made a 90-degree right turn, slid, and came to rest on a bank beside the runway. There were no fatalities, but the aircraft was damaged beyond repair.

Bandeirante Embraer EMB-110P PT-GKU at Belem Airport on April 16, 1982. This aircraft was delivered in December 1976 as PT-GKU (c/n 110131) for VOTEC, which merged with Brasil Central Linhas Aéreas in August 1986. It was wfu at Jacarepaguá–Roberto Marinho Airport in Brazil in May 2009. VOTEC is a third-level airline formed by VOTEC Taxi Aéreo SA and VASP to serve the states of Minas Gerais and Goias in Brazil. The company is also Brazil's largest charter and air taxi company, operating out of all major cities in Brazil.

TABA Fairchild FH-227B PT-LBF at Santarem Airport on April 17, 1982. Delivered to Mohawk Airlines as N7810M (c/n 528) in December 1966, it was transferred to Allegheny Airlines on April 12, 1972, and wfu at Pinal Airpark in Arizona later. Pan Adria Airways purchased the aircraft as YU-ALB in September 1974, and it remained with the company after it became Transadria on September 15, 1978. On April 9, 1980, it was bought by Atlas Aircraft Sales as N851TA, then sold to TABA on September 12, 1980, as PT-LBF. As of 2001, it was wfu at Belem Airport. TABA provides passenger and cargo charters from its main base at Belem Airport with Embraer EMB-110Cs, Fairchild Hiller FH-226Bs, and, in the past, C-46s and Beech D-18s.

FAB PBY-6A FAB-6552 at Manaus AFB on April 17, 1982. Delivered to the United States Navy as Bu 46643 (c/n 2007) on February 20, 1945, it was struck off charge in August 1956. Following this, it was sold to the Aircraft Instrument Corporation in Miami Florida on October 8, 1956, as N9556C, and subsequently bought by Servicio Aereo Vale Amazonico as PT-BBQ. The aircraft was acquired by Panair do Brasil in 1964, and through leasing it was registered to Cruzeiro do Sul on February 10, 1965 as PP-PEB. Panair do Brasil went bankrupt on June 28, 1965, but PP-PEB kept the same license plate from July 1, 1965, until 1971. On December 17, 1971, it was bought by the FAB as FAB-6552 and served until it was withdrawn from use on February 5, 1982, and preserved at the Aeronautical Museum at Belém AFB.

FAB PBY-6A FAB-6552 at Manuas AFB on April 17, 1982. The PBY-6A was withdrawn from use in February 1982, and during the author's visit to Manaus in April 1982, the commander of the base said that the PBY-6A was to be officially removed from duty that August.

Douglas C-47B N259DC at the Brazilian Air Force Aerospace Museum at Afonsos Air Force Base on October 22, 1988. Delivered to the USAAF in 1944 as 43-48690 (c/n 25951), this aircraft was sold to the United States Navy as 17286, then later bought by an unknown owner as N9445. It was sold to the Federal Aviation Administration as N62, reregistered as N69, and then bought by Airplane Sales International Corp as N259DC on October 4, 1985. When the aircraft was transferred to the FAB for flight calibration as FAB-2079, one side painted in the colors of the air force, the other in the colors of the Museu Aeroespacial colors. Purchased by Lineas Aéreas Canedo (LAC) in 1990 as CP-2255, the aircraft was leased to Caribbean Flights as YV-912C in 1992; however the latter ceased operations and YV-912C was wfu and broken up at Valencia Arturo Michelena.

Rio-Sul Fokker F-27-200 PT-LDJ at Rio de Janeiro Santos Dumont Airport on October 24, 1988. Delivered to All Nippon Airways as JA8631 (c/n 10253) on June 17, 1964, it was bought by Trans Australian Airlines as VH-TFW in May 1972, then sold to Rio-Sul in September 1982 as PT-LDJ. In November 1989, it was bought by Pakistan International Airlines as AP-BDQ, and was wfu in July 2006.

PT-LAJ TAM Transportes Aereos Regionais S.A. Fokker F-27-500F at Rio de Janeiro Santos Dumont Airport on October 24, 1988. Delivered to TAM Transportes Aereos Regionais S.A. on January 7, 1983, as PT-LAJ (c/n 10632), it was transferred to TAM Linha Aerea Regional in December 1995. Following this, it was bought by Farner Air Transport in July 1999 as PH-FYC and leased to Tulip Air in September 1999. Sold to Magicbird Airlines in January 2004, it was bought by Farnair Hungary on December 7, 2004 as HA-FAF and stored at Kemble Airport in the UK in September 2010. On August 11, 2011, it was purchased by 19th Hole Inc as N19XF, then by Asialink Cargo Express on March 23, 2012, as PK-KRA. In October 2019, it was stored at Juanda International Airport, Surabaya.

Chapter 4

Paraguay

Lineas Aereas Paraguayas (LAP) Convair CV-240-6 ZP-CDO at Asuncion Airport on January 15, 1979. Delivered to Zonas Oeste y Norte de Aerolineas Argentinas on February 26, 1949, as LV-ADO (c/n 62), it was bought by LAP in November 1962 as ZP-CDO *Gral Bernardino Cabalero*. The aircraft was wfu at Asuncion Airport in 1972, but in May 2022, LAP began work with the local authorities on the CV-240-6's restoration project.

LAP Lockheed L-188C ZP-CBZ at Asuncion Airport January 15, 1979. Delivered to Eastern Air Lines as N5539 (c/n 1080) on August 28, 1959, it was bought by LAP on December 15, 1968. After 23 years of service, it was wfu at Asuncion Airport in 1991. On February 18, 1994, it was sold to New ACS as 9Q-CRR and later bought by TSA in December 1994. On December 18, 1995, TSA pilots were flying the aircraft from N'djili Airport to Angola with 144 passengers on board, approximately 40 passengers over the maximum load. As a consequence, the Electra crashed near Cahungula, in the province of Lunda Norte in Angola. Sadly, there were no survivors.

FAP PBY-5A FAP-2002 at Asuncion Airport on November 18, 1988. Delivered to the United States Navy as Bu 48375 (c/n 1737) on December 15, 1943, it ended its service in August 1953 and was sold to Trans Alaskan Airlines as N4937V in November 1953. Over the next year, it was in service with several other operators, including Foreign & Domestic Enterprises, Flightcraft Inc. and Fleetway Inc. It was bought by Linea Aerea de Transporte Nacional (LATN) in December 1954 as ZP-CBA and was transferred to the TAM Transporte Aereo Militar in 1955 as T-29; it returned to LATN in 1956 and was placed in open storage at Asuncion Airport in November 1957 until 1988. It was sold to Frank Porter on January 19, 1993, and reregistered as N96FP with Frank's Aircraft Sales. In April 1994, the aircraft was bought by Caribbean Air Transport as N96FP and later sold to Universal Associates as N96UC in August 1996, which operated it until 2006. In January 2007, Kermit Weeks' Fantasy of Flight purchased the aircraft, to be based at Polk City in Florida.

Above left: Paraguay Air Force (Fuerza Aérea Paraguaya, FAP) Convair C-131D FAP-2001 at Asuncion Airport on November 18, 1988. Delivered to the United States Air Force (USAF) as 55-0297 (c/n 322) in May 1956 as a Convair VC-131D, it was converted to a Convair C-131D and bought by the FAP as T-93 and reregistered in 1980 as FAP-2001. The Convair was up for sale by 1997, but failed to sell and was broken up at Asuncion Airport by 2005.

Above right: The author recounts a visit to Asuncion: "I have been involved in research of Catalinas for many years, and during my visit to Asuncion Airport in November 1988, a high-ranking officer asked me if I could help create a maintenance instructions manual for a broken FAP Catalina, to which I agreed. LAP had weekly flights from Asuncion Airport to Brussels Airport, so on January 2, 1989, I brought the big maintenance book to the Sheraton Hotel in Brussels where the LAP crews stayed during their stopovers; I handed the manual over to Captain Cesar Rios, and he took it to the LAP and FAP maintenance crews, and a few months later the Catalina was in the air again after a long time on the ground."

Chapter 5

Uruguay

CAUSA Lockheed L-749A CX-BBM at Montevideo Carrasco Airport, Uruguay, in February 1973. The aircraft was delivered to KLM Royal Dutch Airlines as PH-TFE *Utrecht* (c/n 2641) on June 29, 1950, and was reregistered as PH-LDE on March 10, 1954. It was wfu and stored at Schiphol Amsterdam Airport on March 3, 1960, but was sold to CAUSA as CX-BBM on February 5, 1963. On August 29, 1964, it overran the runway at Buenos Aires Aeroparque Airport, due to nose-wheel flutter, but was repaired. CAUSA ceased operations on May 9, 1967, and the aircraft was wfu and stored at Carrasco International Airport; it was broken up during 1973.

Aerotransportes Entre Rios (AER) Lockheed L-749 LV-IGS at Montevideo Carrasco International Airport in February 1973. Delivered to KLM Royal Dutch Airlines as PH-TEP (c/n 2540) on August 13, 1947, it was reregistered as PH-LDR on March 16, 1954. In September 1960, SALA fitted the aircraft with a cargo door in the forward fuselage and then returned it to Schiphol Amsterdam Airport, where the registration was cancelled on February 18, 1964. Two days later, it was reregistered as TI-1044P and then again as LV-IGS in April 1964 for AER. It was stored at Buenos Aires Ezeiza Airport in March 1967, but re-entered service in July 1970. In January 1973, the aircraft was bought by another operator in ex-AER colours, stored and wfu at Montevideo Carrasco, and broken up in January 1982.

Chapter 6

Argentina

Aerolineas Argentinas Avro 748 Srs 1/105 LV-HHC at Buenos Aires Aeroparque Airport on November 14, 1973. Delivered to Aerolineas Argentinas on April 24, 1962, as LV-PRJ (c/n 1541), it was reregistered as LV-HHC on April 25, 1962. The aircraft was bought by Dan-Air as G-BEKC on February 10, 1977, and wfu and stored at Manchester Airport in December 1987; it was broken up at Manchester Airport in 1989.

Austral Lineas Aereas NAMC YS-11A-309 LV-JLJ at Buenos Aires Aeroparque Airport on November 14, 1973. The aircraft was first flown on November 28, 1968 and first delivered to Austral Lineas Aereas on June 10, 1969, as LV-JLJ (c/n 2088). It was bought by Lineas Aereas del Estado in 1979 as LV-JLJ and then sold to Fuji Heavy Industries as JA-8832 in April 1983. Mid Pacific Air bought the aircraft in June 1983 as N124MP, and it was converted to freighter standard on January 3, 1990 for KOA Holdings. It was wfu in 1994 and bought by KFS Aviation in 1997. On February 19, 2013, it was scrapped at Lafayette Purdue Field, Indiana.

PLUNA Vickers Viscount V.769D CX-AQN at Buenos Aires Aeroparque Airport on November 14, 1973. Delivered to PLUNA on May 13, 1958, as CX-AQN (c/n 321) from Weybridge, Surrey, it stayed with the company until it was bought by Ronald J. Clark in May 1982 as N410RC. It was sold to Jadepoint in January 1988, stored at Tucson Airport without engines or titles, and broken up during 1990.

Argentine Naval Prefecture Short Skyvan SC7-3M-400 PA-51 at Buenos Aires Aeroparque Airport on November 14, 1973. Delivered to the Argentine Navy on June 2, 1971, with c/n SH.1888, it was sold to CAE Aviation as LX-ABC on August 24, 1989. It was subsequently bought by GB Airlink as N80GB on January 17, 2003, and based at Fort Lauderdale, Florida; it was still active during 2008.

Aerolíneas Colonia Convair CV-240-0 CX-BHT at Buenos Aires Aeroparque Airport on November 14, 1973. Delivered to American Airlines as N94210 (c/n 18) on November 19, 1948, it was subsequently bought by the Dundel Corporation on December 31, 1957, and then sold to Cruziero do Sol as PP-CEW on May 19, 1958. Following this, it was bought by the Aircraft Sales Corporation in November 1967 as N21118 and leased to Copa Panama as HP-471 on January 30, 1968, returning on March 20, 1969. The Charlotte Aircraft Corporation purchased the aircraft on June 6, 1969, followed by TRAFE, which bought it as LV-PQK in November 1970. It was leased to Aerolineas Colonia as LV-JTI in 1970, then sold to ARCO a few months later as CX-BHT. It was wfu, stored and broken up at Colonia Airport in Uruguay during 1974.

Argentine Air Force (Fuerza Aérea Argentina, FAA) Douglas C-47A TC-33 arriving at Buenos Aires Aeroparque Airport on November 14, 1973. This aircraft was delivered to the USAAF as 43-15327 (c/n 20093), on April 18, 1944, and was sold later as N67776. Wasserman purchased the aircraft as LV-NQU on May 26, 1947, and sold it on to the FAA as T-67 on August 7, 1948. Registrations with the FAA included T-04, TC-04, E-304, and TC-33 in December 1969. It ended up at the Aeroclub at Baradero, Argentina, in January 2002.

FAA Fokker F-27-600 T-44 arriving at Buenos Aires Aeroparque Airport, on November 14, 1973. First flown on November 29, 1971, as PH-EXB, this aircraft was delivered to Lineas Aereas del Estado as T-44 on December 28, 1971. Sixteen F-27 aircraft, of various models, have been delivered to the Lineas Aereas del Estado since 1968, for use by the IV Escuadron de Transporte. Lineas Aereas del Estado aircraft, which are controlled by the I Brigade, are flown and serviced by air force personnel but have civilian cabin attendants, and operations come under the supervision of the Department of Civil Aviation. T-44's last operational report was in 2008, and following this it was most likely used for spares and abandoned in Comodoro Rivadavia International Airport, probably broken up.

Austral Lineas Aereas Curtiss C-46A LV-FSA at Buenos Aires Aeroparque Airport on November 16, 1973. Delivered to the USAAF as 42-96661 (c/n 30323) on August 3, 1944, this aircraft transferred to the United States Navy as 39546 in the same month, later being stored as N3943A at Litchfield Park in Arizona in December 1946. Aerovias Monder bought it as LV-PBH, then changed the registration to become LV-FSA on October 6, 1956. It was transferred to Austral on December 23, 1957, and leased to Aervias Halcon in 1968. Aircraft Line Maintenance in Miami, Florida, purchased it on July 30, 1979 as N8040Y; on its ferry flight to Miami via Chile and Panama on August 4, 1979, the aircraft was crossing the Andes mountains near Tupungato Peak when it crashed into a glacier, breaking into three. Tragically, all five crew were killed, and the wreckage was found in 1981 by a Chilean SAR team that was looking for a missing helicopter. (R. M. Collection)

AER Canadair CL-44-6 LV-JSY (Canadair CC-106 Yukon) at Buenos Aires Ezeiza Airport on November 15, 1973. Delivered to the Royal Canadian Air Force (RCAF) as 15925 (c/n 5) on May 23, 1961, it was re-serialled as 106925 on February 1, 1968. The aircraft was sold to AER in November 1970 as LV-PQL and reregistered as LV-JSY on November 12, 1970. On September 27, 1975, it was written off during take-off at Miami Airport when the CL-44 hit the runway and splashed into a canal nearby. Six of the ten people aboard were killed, but two crew and two passengers survived the crash.

Transporte Aereo Rioplatense Canadair CL-44D4-6 LV-JZM at Buenos Aires Ezeiza Airport on November 13, 1973. The aircraft was delivered on September 25, 1962 as N604SA (c/n 32) to Slick Airways, which merged with Airlift International on July 1, 1966. It was leased to Trans Mediterranean in November 1967, returned in May 1968, and was subsequently bought by International Air Leases Inc in 1972. Transporte Aereo Rioplatense purchased the aircraft as LV-JZM in May 1972, and by May 1980, it was wfu, stored and broken up at Buenos Aires Ezeiza Airport.

Aerolineas Uruguayas Fairchild F-27J CX-BPP at Buenos Aires Aeroparque Airport leaving on October 28, 1988. Delivered to Allegheny Airlines as N2705J (c/n 116) in November 1965, it was bought by Air South on December 23, 1974, and subsequently sold to Artnell International on April 17, 1975. LANSA purchased it as HR-LAP in May 1978, stored and wfu at Miami Airport, then sold it to the Government Assisted Finance Association in October 1982 as N275PH. It was leased to Horizon Airlines on October 13, 1982, sold to an unknown buyer in March 1984, then bought by de Havilland Canada in September 1986. It was sold to Boeing Equipment Holding Corporation in November 1987 and then bought by Aerolineas Uruguayas in January 1988 as CX-BPP. On July 27, 1993, was wfu and stored at Aeroparque Airport and scrapped during January 1990.

Gobierno de Entre Ríos FMA IA-50 Guarani II LV-LAE at Buenos Aires Aeroparque Airport on October 28, 1988. The IA-50 was an Argentine twin turboprop light transport aircraft for 12 to 15 passengers. It was designed by Hector E. Ruiz for the Military Aircraft Factory in Argentina; 35 were built, and this image shows c/n 27. The aircraft was damaged beyond repair on January 23, 1994, at Santa Elena airstrip, when the main undercarriage collapsed rearwards during touchdown.

CATA Linea Aerea Fairchild F-27J LV-AZV at Buenos Aires Aeroparque Airport on October 29, 1988. This aircraft (c/n 65) was delivered to Bonanza Air Lines as N150L in October 1959 as a model F-27A, and was reregistered as N750L in 1964. Bonanza merged with Air West in March 1968 and sold N750L to Hughes Air West. From there, it was bought by Air Mauritanie as 5T-CJU on June 26, 1974, and after almost 10 years of service it was sold to Scott Kidwell in February 1984 as N4798W. Next it was bought by Horizon Airlines in May 1984, reregistered as N280PH in July 1984, and converted from an F-27A to an F-27J in December 1985. In January 1987, it was wfu and stored at Las Vegas Airport in Nevada until it was bought by CATA in July 1987 as LV-PAD, and reregistered as LV-AZV in November 1987. It was wfu again in 2002 and dismantled; the fuselage and tail are now at a technical college near Buenos Aires Aeroparque Airport.

CATA Linea Aerea IAI Arava 201 LV-OLS at Buenos Aires Aeroparque Airport, October 29, 1988. Founded in 1986, CATA ceased operations in 2006; the company had five Fairchild FH-227s and one IAI Arava in its fleet. Delivered to Israel Aircraft Industries Ltd as 4X-IBS (c/n 46), the aircraft was purchased by CATA as LV-PIJ in September 1980 and reregistered it as LV-OLS in October 1980. After 20 years of service, LV-OLS was sold to Win Win Aviation in October 2001 as N302CL, and subsequently reregistered to Owl Aerospace at North Miami Beach.

Argentine Navy (Armada Argentina) Douglas C-47 A5-T-22, Ushuaia-Comandante Berisso air base on November 3, 1988. Delivered to the USAAF as Bu 42-23716 (c/n 9578), the aircraft was bought by the Argentine Navy as 2-GT-15 for Sqn No 2 in December 1946. It was reregistered as 2-GT-9 in January 1948, and by 1952 was serving with Sqn No 4 as 4-T-22. It returned to Sqn No 2 as CTA-22 in 1965 for the Air Naval Transport Command (Comando de Transportes Aeronavales) and was then transferred to the Mobile Logistics Support Squadron (Escuadrilla de Sosten Logistico Movil) at Cape Horn (Cabo de Hornos). Its last service flight was on July 28, 1979, after which it was restored and put on display at the Aero-Club Ushuaia in full Argentine Navy colours. Ushuaia claims the title of the world's southernmost city. It also marks the end of the very long highway that runs over 3,000km to Buenos Aires. These days, its main industry is tourism, serving as gateway to Antarctica.

FAA Fokker F-27-500 TC-75 flying for Lineas Aereas del Estado at Ushuaia Airport on November 4, 1988. Its first flight was on November 8, 1981, as PH-EXM (c/n 10621), and it was delivered to the FAA on December 18, 1981, as TC-75. Its last operational report was in August 2013, and in 2016 it was observed inside a hangar at Parana Airport in the Entre Rios province with many parts missing and no engines; at some point, it is believed to have been used in a fire drill.

On November 4, 1988, FAA Fokker F-27-500 TC-75 is flying for Lineas Aereas del Estado, and boarding at Ushuaia Airport for a flight to El Calafate with stops at Rio Grande and Rio Gallegos. In the background, there is an Argentina Navy Lockheed L-188PF with the serial 5-T-3.

Argentine National Gendarmerie (Gendarmería Nacional Argentina) Pilatus PC-6/B2-H4 Turbo Porter GN-807 (c/n 805) at Río Gallegos Airport, November 4, 1988. It first flew in 1979, with the Flight Operations Support Division at Rio Gallegos Airport. On July 9, 2000, it crashed at Tarde airstrip in the Gobernador Gregores area; the crew escaped unhurt and the aircraft was rebuilt.

FAA Fokker F-27-500 TC-75 arriving at El Calafate airstrip on November 4, 1988; it is the gateway to the Los Glaciares National Park, home to Lago Argentino and the Perito Moreno glacier, in the Patagonian province of Santa Cruz.

Lago Argentino and the Perito Moreno glacier in the Patagonian province of Santa Cruz, November 5, 1988.

Chapter 7

Chile

Aeroservicio Parrague Ltda Consolidated PBY-6A ASPAR CC-CNP arriving at Santiago Los Cerrillos Airport on November 19, 1973. Delivered to the United States Navy as 46665 (c/n 2029) on March 22, 1945, it was struck off charge in August 1956. Following this, it was sold to the Aircraft Instrument Corporation in 1956 as N9555C; to TRANSA-Chile as CC-CNG in 1957; ASPAR in 1959 as CC-CNP; and then leased to ICONA in Spain in July 1988 for firefighting duties. The 8,000-mile flight to its new home with ICONA began with two Catalinas, CC-CNP and CC-CDT, on June 25, 1988, via Mendoza in Argentina, Asuncion, Campo Grande, Brasilia, Recife and Fernando do Noronha in Brazil, Dakar in Senegal, Las Palmas, Madrid and finally, on July 8, 1988, Zaragoza in Spain. CC-CNP became EC-FXN for Andalusian Aerial Fumigation (Fumigacion Aerea Andaluza, FAASA) on July 1, 1994. It returned to the CC-CNP registration in 1998 for Aerocondor, and was stored at Pinhancos in Portugal from 2001 until 2002. It was sold to the Catalina Flying Memorial Ltd in Australia on July 27, 2007 as VH-CAT, departed Portugal to Australia in November 2008, and arrived at Sydney Bankstown Airport on December 7, 2008.

Lineas Aereas Sud Americana Curtiss C-46D CC-CDC at Santiago Los Cerrillos Airport, November 19, 1973. Delivered to the USAAF as Bu 42-101198 (c/n 30653) on October 16, 1944, it was bought by the Indian government on April 10, 1946, and was then wfu and stored at New Delhi Airport. In October 1954, it was sold to Borges Tillotson Aircraft as N68851, and then bought by Lidca Colombia in July 1956 as HK-829. It was sold to Transa Chile as CC-CND in 1957, and then bought by Lineas Aereas Sud Americana in 1963 as CC-CDC. The aircraft was wfu and stored at Miami Airport Florida until it was purchased by Victor Salas in 1975, which also stored the aircraft, but this time at Opa-Locka Airport, Florida, in 1976. In 1984, Servicios Aereos R.D. purchased it as HP-977, then sold it to Haiti Air Freight in 1986 as HH-DGA. After being wfu and stored at Miami Airport, the aircraft was bought by the Museum of Aviation at Robins AFB in Georgia, in August 1991, as 42-101198.

Linea Aerea Del Cobre Ltda (LADECO) Douglas C-47-DL CC-CAO at Santiago Los Cerrillos Airport on November 19, 1973. Delivered to the USAAF as 41-7740 (c/n 4219) on February 24, 1942, this aircraft was bought by a private owner as NC54088, then reregistered as N77C for the Pressed Steel Car Corp. The latter sold it to LADECO in June 1963 as CC-CAO, which subsequently sold it on to an unknown owner as N783V on March 4, 1976. It was bought by Tol-Air Services Inc at Rio Piedras in Puerto Rico as N783T on June 15, 1990, and sold to Sky Charter Inc from Opa-Locka Airport as N783T on June 13, 1997. MBD Corp operated the aircraft from San Juan Airport from October 25, 2000, as N783T, but the registration was cancelled on March 20, 2018, and it was left to become derelict at Opa-Locka.

Solastral Douglas DC-6B(F) CC-CDH *Cabo de Hornaos* at Santiago Los Cerrillos Airport on November 19, 1973, still in the old paint of the previous owner, Loftleider, from Iceland. Delivered to Pan American World Airways as a DC-6B on April 4, 1954, as N6117C (c/n 44117) this aircraft was bought by Loftleider on August 12, 1961, as TF-LLD, then sold to Solastral in July 1968 as CC-CDH and converted to DC-6B(F) standard. Solastral rebranded as Trans Global in June 1974, and sold CC-CDH to Aeronica from Nicaragua as YN-BVI in April 1980 with the name *Cmdte Pomares*. The aircraft was taking off at Panama City Tocumen Airport on October 6, 1980, when the nose gear collapsed and it was damaged beyond repair.

Chilean Aeronautic Authorities Douglas C-47A A1-971 at Santiago Los Cerrillos Airport on November 18, 1973. Delivered to the USAAF as 41-7684 (c/n 4148) on August 2, 1941, it went to civil registry as NC-84 on April 30, 1946. The registration was changed to N24 on April 24, 1952, and the aircraft was sold to the FAA on December 21, 1958. It was subsequently sold to the Chilean Air Force (Fuerza Aérea de Chile) as 971 in 1964. Chilean Aeronautic Authorities operated the aircraft as A1-971 from April 1971 to February 1980, then sold it to Aircraft Holdings Inc in Miami on November 8, 1982, where it was registered as N2782S in June 1983. It was wfu at an unknown location.

LAN Chile CC-CCF Douglas DC-6B 403 at Santiago Los Cerrillos Airport on November 18, 1973. Delivered to LAN Chile on March 17, 1955, as CC-GLDC (c/n 44692), it was reregistered as CC-CCF in 1956, then wfu and stored at Santiago Los Cerrillos 1973. It was purchased by Linea Aerea Sud Americana as CC-CCF in 1974, and wfu at Santiago Los Cerrillos airport in 1982.

LADECO Douglas DC-6B(F) CC-CEV at Santiago Los Cerrillos Airport on November 19, 1973. Delivered to Canadian Pacific Airlines as CF-CZE (c/n 44891) on January 16, 1956, this aircraft was converted from a DC-6B to a DC-6B(F) cargo in 1960 and was bought by World Airways on November 1, 1961, as N45502. It was sold to LADECO in April 1972 as CC-CEV, then bought by Cia de Renta la Portena in May 1979 as CC-PJG. LADECO withdrew it and stored it at Santiago Los Cerrillos Airport before selling it to Atlas Aircraft Corporation on July 19, 1979, as N841TA. Next, it was transferred to Trans Air Link Corporation in August 1982, leased to Southern Air Transport in April 1983 and returned in 1984. Trans Air Supply purchased the aircraft in February 1996, and it was stored at Melbourne Airport, Florida, in October 1998, and wfu in October 2003. The nose and front fuselage were donated to the 1940 Air Terminal Museum in Houston, Texas.

LAN CHILE Avro/Hawker Siddeley HS 748 Srs 2/234 CC-CEF in Puerto Williams Airport on November 18, 1973. This aircraft (c/n 1617) was delivered to LAN CHILE on December 15, 1967, then converted to an Srs 2A/234 and bought by Austin Airways as C-GQTH in May 1979. It was leased to Maersk Air as OY-MBH from December 1980 until March 1981, and after returning was sold to Ilford-Riverton Airways in 1984. Ilford-Riverton changed its name to Northland Air Manitoba on February 13, 1986, and sold the aircraft to Nunasi-Northland Airways in February 1989. The 748 crashed during take-off on November 10, 1993, 2km northwest of Sandy Lake in Ontario, and was damaged beyond repair; sadly, there were seven fatalities. (R. M. Collection)

Aeronavale Catalina OA-10A 20 at Cerrillos Airport on November 14, 1988. It was delivered to the USAAF as 44-34009 (c/n CV520) on December 12, 1944, then struck off charge on April 12, 1947. The aircraft was sold to H. Hocket from Honolulu in 1948 as NC62043, and after this, the aircraft passed through many operators, including Ryan Oil, Lund Aviation, Wheeler Airlines, Timmins Aviation, and Union de Transports Aerien in February 1966. It transferred to the Aeronaval as No 20 on March 9, 1966, to be based at Papeete, Tahiti, in support of French atomic testing. Its last flight was on November 28, 1971, and it was wfu from 1971 till 1973, then donated along with two others to Chile; the Catalinas were shipped from Papeete to Valparaiso in August 1973, then flown to Santiago Los Cerrillos Airport in November 1974. ASPAR purchased the aircraft as CC-CDU on January 10, 1975, and, after being wfu and stripped for spares, it was moved to the Museo Nacional de Aeronautica de Chile in April 1995 and displayed as FAC-405 in December 2006. (R. M. Collection)

ASPAR PBY-6A CC-CCS *Tanker 34* at Santiago Los Cerrillos Airport on November 14, 1988. Delivered to the United States Navy as 46678 (c/n 2043) on October 4, 1945, it was struck off charge in August 1956, and then sold to the Aircraft Instrument Corporation as N9562C on October 8, 1956. TRANSA-Chile purchased the aircraft as CC-CNF in 1957, and subsequently transferred it to ASPAR as CC-CCS in April 1980. It was converted to fire tanker no 34, and, while on duty, struck a rock during a water landing in Lake Gutierez, Argentina. The aircraft was salvaged and trucked to Santiago for rebuilding. Once repaired, it was leased to ICONA in Spain and delivered on July 6, 1991 to Palma del Rio, after which it was wfu at Pinhancos Airport in Portugal from 2001 to 2002. It was sold to HARS from Australia as VH-PBZ, and delivered to Australia on September 9, 2003, although it did not arrive in Darwin until September 21, where it was repainted in an RAAF black wartime scheme as A24-362.

Aero Sur Patagonia Fairchild F-27F ASA CC-CAS at El Tepual International Airport, Puerto Montt, on November 11, 1988, having arrived from Punta Arenas. Delivered to L. S. Rockefeller as N2726R (c/n 99) on December 22, 1963, it was sold to the Wayfarer Ketch Corporation on January 21, 1964 and then bought by Time Life Inc on June 21, 1971. It was reregistered as N630TL on August 30, 1971, then sold to Med-Air International in May 1987. Aeroregional leased the aircraft in June 1987 and reregistered it as CC-CAS in August 1987, returning it to Med-Air on March 29, 1994. It was then leased to Aero Sur Patagonia on the same day, and sold to Air Atlantic Uruguay as CX-BRT in December 1994. Anstan Lineas Aerea bought the F-27F in 2001, but it was not taken up, so it was instead transferred to Alas Del Sur. It was wfu at Viru Viru International Airport, Bolivia, as CP-2479, and was still there as of 2019.

Chapter 8

Bolivia

Horizontes Douglas C-47A CP-728 at La Paz El Alto Airport on November 21, 1973. Delivered to the USAF as 43-15223 (c/n 19689) in 1944, it went to Yacimientos Petroleros Fiscales Bolivianos as CP-728, and was then bought by Transportes Aereos Itanez in 1973. The aircraft was destroyed in a belly landing on January 6, 1977, during a flight from Santa Cruz Airport to Trinidad Airport, near La Senda Portachicalo, Bolivia; thankfully, there were no fatalities.

Bolivian Airways North American B-25D Mitchell CP-915 at La Paz El Alto Airport on November 21, 1973. This aircraft was delivered to the RCAF as 5230 and Bu 43-3308 on January 5, 1945, and was struck off charge on November 22, 1961. Sold as N8011 to a private owner, it was reregistered as HP-428 for Aerovias Internacional Alianza in 1966, then bought by Transportes Aereos Benianos as CP-915 in April 1970. It was sold to Sudamericana and then transferred to Bolivian Airways in December 1972, and in 1973 was wfu at La Paz El Alto Airport. Private buyer Roy Stafford from Jacksonville, Florida, was the next owner, and the B-25D was shipped to the US in 1987. The aircraft was restored in Chino, California, as PBJ-1D for the Marine Corps Air-Ground Museum at Quantico, Virginia, in 1988.

Aerolineas Comerciales Nacionales Alcon Douglas DC-6B(F) CP-947 at La Paz El Alto Airport on November 21, 1973. Delivered to KLM Royal Dutch Airlines as PH-TGA (c/n 44076) on July 18, 1953, it was reregistered as PH-DFA on February 16, 1954. Nevado Aero Trades purchased the aircraft on May 12, 1960, as N6574C and leased it to Trans American Airlines on May 13, 1960. In August 1960, it was leased to Great Lakes Airlines, returning in May 1961 to be leased further to Trans Alaskan Airlines on May 6, 1961, and Admiral Air Service in December 1961. It was bought by Twentieth Century Aircraft in 1963 and sold to Zantop Air Transport on June 19, 1964, which became Universal Airlines in 1966. It was then sold to the Boreas Corporation in 1967; Span East Airlines as N611SE in January 1970; Quanama West Indies Co on July 31, 1970; and Alcon in August 1971 as CP-947. On February 6, 1974, it was damaged beyond repair at Bolivia's San Juan Airport when the No. 4 engine caught fire on take-off. The DC-6B(F) landed normally but veered left after 950m and ran off the runway, coming to rest 80m from the runway edge with its nosegear collapsed; there were no fatalities.

Cooperativa Aerea de Transportes Ltd (CADET) Douglas DC-3/DST CP-572 at La Paz El Alto Airport on November 21, 1973. Delivered to American Airlines as NC16007 in August 1936, this was the 12th Douglas DST-144 (Douglas Sleeper Transport) out of a total of 21 made. It was converted to Douglas C-49E standard in March 1943 for the USAAF and reregistered as 42-56094 (c/n 1549). It returned to American Airlines as NC16007 in November 1944 and was wfu in May 1949. SANTA Ecuador purchased the aircraft in August 1949 as HC-SMB, and then sold it to Lloyd Aereo Boliviano (LAB) as CB-72 in January 1951, after which it was reregistered as CP-572 on October 10, 1953. On September 5, 1955, it was damaged near Cochabamba in a mid-air collision with an LAB B-17 (CP-597); the DC-3 landed without loss of life, but the B-17 crashed and three crew members died. It was bought by CADET in November 1969, sold to Cargo Aerea Transportade as CP-572 in 1975, and broken up in 1977 at an unknown location.

North American B-25J Mitchell CP-808 at La Paz El Alto Airport on November 21, 1973. Built originally for the RCAF as Bu 86820 (serial 5204), on July 6, 1951, it was later bought by a private owner as N92874, and then sold on to the Quick Freeze Corp in Saint Thomas, US Virgin Islands, as N232S in 1963. Curtiss National Bank in Miami purchased the aircraft in 1966, later selling it to F. Garcia from La Paz as CP-808 in April 1967. It crashed at Itagua in Bolivia on April 19, 1967, but, seemingly repaired, it was bought by Bolivariana in 1972, only to crash again at an unknown location on November 21, 1977.

Frigorificos Movima (FRIMO) Convair CV-440-59 CP-961 at La Paz El Alto Airport on November 21, 1973. Delivered to Cruzeiro do Sol as PP-CEO *Pollux* (c/n 467) in February 1958, it was bought by the Charlotte Aircraft Corporation in October 1967 as N21467, wfu and stored at an unknown location, then bought by FRIMO in February 1972 as CP-961. On January 7, 1975, during a flight from San Borja Airport to La Paz El Alto Airport, the right powerplant encountered a fuel leak; the crew decided to return to San Borja, because the CV-440 was losing height rapidly, but as the San Borja radio aid was unserviceable, the crew made a precautionary landing in flat terrain. The tail of the Convair separated and the aircraft came to rest in flames; one of the passengers was killed while 28 other occupants were injured and evacuated. The Convair was written off.

FRIMO Curtiss C-46D CP-777 at La Paz El Alto Airport during some maintenance on November 21, 1973. Delivered to the USAAF on March 23, 1945 as 44-78083 (c/n 33479), it was transferred to the Reconstruction Finance Corporation on January 16, 1946. It was wfu and stored at Walnut Ridge Airport in Arkansas until being purchased by Andesa as HC-SCJ in 1946. Next, it was sold to the Linda Susan Corporation in 1949 as N3947C; bought by Modern Air Transport in 1953; sold to Aerovias Panama as HP-325 in 1961; bought by Aerolineas Domingo Erregaborda as LV-PGJ in December 1965; and sold to Transaereos Frimo on July 13, 1967, which became FRIMO in 1971. On December 23, 1979, on approach to La Paz El Alto Airport, the C-46D struck the slope of a mountain located 15km from La Paz El Alto; the Curtiss was destroyed and all three crew members were killed.

Trans Aereos Illimani Curtiss CP-910 C-46D at La Paz El Alto Airport on November 21, 1973. The USAAF received this aircraft as 44-77838 (c/n 33234) in 1945, and it received civil registration N32228 on February 3, 1965. It was stored at Davis-Monthan AFB, Arizona, until it was bought by Parts Incorporation from Miami Springs, Florida, in April 1969, and then sold to Aerovias Las Minas in 1970 as CP-910. Finally, it was transferred to Trans Aereo Illimani in 1972. On December 7, 1973, while flying from an unknown destination to Santa Ana del Yacuma Airport in the Beni Department, the Curtiss caught fire and was destroyed after landing; there were no fatalities. This image was taken just two weeks ago before the crash.

Frigorifico Reyes Boeing B-17G Flying Fortress CP-891 at La Paz El Alto Airport on November 21, 1973. Delivered to the USAAF as 44-6393 (c/n 22616) on July 20, 1944, it was allocated to 15th Air Force in Italy in August 1944 and spent 10 months in combat in Europe. It spent the next 11 years as a VIP aircraft at Olmstead in Florida, also serving with the 18th Maintenance & Supply Group at Clark AFB in the Philippines, and with the 1130th Special Activities Group at Nanking in China. In June 1956, it was taken from the USAF surplus and given to the Bolivian government as CP-627, where it was subsequently transferred to LAB in January 1957. On August 27, 1968, it crashed on approach at La Paz El Alto Airport, but was rebuilt from another B-17G airframe, 43-38322 CP-580 (c/n 9300) which had crashed in 1965. The rebuilt aircraft was registered as CP-891, and transferred to Frigorifico Reyes during September 1969.

Servicios Aéreos Bolivianos (SAB) Curtiss C-46F CP-990 at La Paz El Alto Airport on November 21, 1973. This aircraft was delivered to the USAAF as 44-78667 (c/n 22490) and bought by Aaxico Airlines on May 15, 1956, as N4718N. It was leased to Northeast Airlines from April 1957 until October 1957, and then to Slick Airways and Zantop Air Transport from late 1957 until June 1963. When it returned, it was exported to Bolivia on August 4, 1969 as CP-795, and reregistered as CP-990 for SAB. On January 6, 1974, during a cargo flight from San Borja Airport to La Paz El Alto Airport, the C-46F struck a mountain near Unduavi and was damaged beyond repair; there were no survivors.

LAB Fairchild F-27M CP-863 at La Paz El Alto Airport on November 21, 1973. Initially registered to Fairchild on February 8, 1968, as N2737R (c/n 128), it was delivered to LAB on July 31, 1969 as CP-863, remaining in service with the airline until 1983. The Oklahoma Aircraft Corporation purchased the aircraft on March 4, 1983, as N276PH, and leased it to Horizon Airlines on the same date. It was bought by Horizon Airlines in March 1984, then sold to de Havilland Canada in September 1986 and leased back to Horizon Airlines on the same date. It was bought by the Boeing Equipment Holding Corporation in November 1987, then sold to William D. Seidle in December 1988, who leased it to Airlift International that same month. The aircraft was reregistered as N276RD in June 1989, and then wfu in July 1991 at Miami Airport. It was damaged beyond repair by Hurricane Andrew on August 24, 1992, and broken up in October 1993.

SAB Curtiss C-46D at La Paz El Alto Airport CP-540 on November 21, 1973. Delivered to the USAAF as 44-78198 (c/n 33594) on April 16, 1945, it was bought by the Corporacion Boliviana de Fomento (CBF) as CB-40 in 1948, and then reregistered as CP-540 in 1951. It was sold to LAB on March 29, 1965, but was not taken up and was transferred to Bolivian Air System on December 22, 1965. It was repossessed by the CBF in 1972, and bought by SAB in 1973 as CP-540. On February 1, 1977, during a cargo flight from Cochabamba Jorge Wilstermann Airport, the Curtiss C-46D suffered an engine failure and the crew attempted an emergency landing. The Curtiss crashed in a wooded area, but luckily both pilots only sustained minor injuries.

La Paz Aerolineas Douglas C-47-DL CP-755 at La Paz El Alto Airport on November 21, 1973. Delivered to the USAAF as 41-7802 (c/n 4294) on April 28, 1942, it was bought by Coastal Air Lines as NC74620 on October 3, 1947, then reregistered to Aaxico American Air Export & Import Co as N74620. It was sold to Aerolineas Abaroa in June 1954 as CP-755, bought by Boliviana de Aviación in 1969, then sold to Aerolineas La Paz in 1975. On November 23, 1976, following a wrong approach at La Paz El Alto Airport, the C-47-DL landed too far down the runway, about 450m past the runway threshold, at an excessive speed of 130kts. On touchdown, the right tyre burst, and the pilot lost control as the aircraft veered off the runway and came to rest; all four crew members were safe, but the C-47-DL was damaged beyond repair.

Bolivian Overseas Airways (BOA) Consolidated C-87 Liberator CP-576 at La Paz El Alto Airport on November 26, 1973. Built as a B-24M Liberator with serial 44-41916 (c/n 5824), it later received the civil registration as N4907L and was bought by Boliviana de Aviacion as CB-76 on March 22, 1951. It transferred to BOA in 1966 as CP-576 and was converted to a Consolidated C-87 Liberator, becoming one of the two rare C-87 Liberators that transported meat, oil and cargo across the Bolivian mountains until as late as 1971. It was wfu at the Frigorifico Reyes ramp at La Paz El Alto Airport in 1973 and stripped for spares. In 1980, the US Air Force Museum acquired it, and the following year it was shipped to Houston and eventually to Castle AFB in California. From 1982 until 1989, parts were gathered and 30,000 volunteer hours were spent reassembling the Liberator; it was rolled out in November 1989 in the colors of the 93rd Bomb Group's *Shady Lady*, and remains on display at Castle Air Museum's air park.

BOA Douglas C-47B CP-720 at La Paz El Alto Airport on November 26, 1973, derelict at the Frigorifico Reyes ramp. Delivered to the USAAF as 45-1081 (c/n 34351) in 1945, it was bought by LAB in August 1945 as CB-30 and reregistered as CP-530 on October 1, 1953. It was sold to Global Aero Service Inc on September 29, 1961 as N343G, and reregistered to the Boreas Corp on November 7, 1961. The registration was later cancelled, and the aircraft was bought by Compania Boliviana de Aviacion in February 1963 as CP-720. It was transferred to Aerolineas Abaroa, which merged with BOA in 1968, and left to become derelict at La Paz El Alto Airport by 1972.

Boliviana de Aviación Consolidated C-87 Liberator CP-787 at La Paz El Alto Airport on November 26, 1973. Delivered to the USAAF as a B-24M with serial 44-50801, it later received the civil registration N299A and was converted to a C-87. It was bought by Boliviana de Aviación in April 1956 as CP-611, but was damaged at Trinidad Airport in Bolivia on March 27, 1964. Once repaired, it was repurchased by Boliviana de Aviación in 1966 as CP-787, then wfu in 1972 and stored at the Frigorifico Reyes ramp at La Paz El Alto Airport. It was broken up in 1975.

Frigorifico Reyes Boeing B-17E CP-753 *Super Tigre* at La Paz El Alto Airport on November 26, 1973. Delivered to the USAAF as 41-9210 (c/n 2682) on May 16, 1942 and bought by Lysdale Flying service as N5842N on August 29, 1952, the aircraft then transferred to Leeward Aeronautical Service on December 3, 1952. It was sold to Kenting Aviation as CF-ICB on March 4, 1955, then bought by Four Star Aviation as N9720F on June 22, 1964. The aircraft was purchased by Boliviana de Aviación as CP-753 on July 23, 1964, then registered to Frigorifico Reyes in November 1964. It was damaged in a take-off accident at San Borja Airport in August 1976, but was repaired for a ferry flight to La Paz El Alto Airport where it was wfu and stored. It was restored to full flying condition in 1990 and bought by World Jet Inc from Fort Laudedale, Florida, and ferried from La Paz El Alto to Fort Lauderdale in March 1990 as N8WJ. It was sold in 1998 to the Flying Heritage Collection of Bellevue in the state of Washington, and flown from Fort Lauderdale to Moses Lake Airport, Washington, in 2004, where it was reregistered as N12355. Ownership then passed to the Vulcan Warbirds from Seattle, a company associated with the Flying Heritage Collection.

"On November 26, 1973, Frigorifico Reyes Boeing B-17E CP-753 was just arriving from Trinidad Airport, Bolivia, during my visit to La Paz El Alto. The crew invited me for a trip to Trinidad the next day, but I had already booked my trip to Peru by steam train and steamer across Lake Titicaca, from Guaqui. Instead, the crew gave a tour of the aircraft and later posed for this photo with the B-17E; in the middle is Captain Gregorio Marowski, and the one on the right was Mr Palenque, Head of Mechanics for Frigorifico Reyes, sadly the name of the man on the left is unknown."

Left: The cockpit of Frigorifico Reyes Boeing B-17E CP-753 on November 26, 1973. The B-17E had a modern look to it and a unique throttle quadrant.

Below: CP-960 FRIMO Curtiss C-46A arriving at La Paz El Alto Airport on November 25, 1974. Delivered to the USAAF as 43-47015 (c/n 00086) on October 16, 1944, it transferred to the United States Marine Corp in November 1944 as 39591 and was sold to the L. B. Smith Aircraft Corporation as N4164A in 1956. It was bought by Transair Sweden as SE-CFC on July 5, 1957 and leased to the United Nations Operation in the Congo from December 30, 1960, until October 18, 1961, and then again from April 15, 1964, until December 1965. Paraense of Brasil purchased the aircraft as PP-BUA in May 1967, and in September 1970 it was wfu at Miami Airport. It was subsequently sold to International Export & Import Co as N9020 in December 1970, then seized by U.S. Customs and Border Protection in February 1971. Transaereos Frimo bought it in 1971 as CP-960, and it was subsequently transferred to FRIMO in January 1972. On February 2, 1975, the undercarriage collapsed during a take-off run at Reyes Airport in the north of Bolivia and the aircraft sustained serious damage. It was wfu and stored at La Paz El Alto Airport in October 1977.

Transporte Aéreo Militar (TAM) Convair CV-580 TAM 70 arriving at La Paz El Alto Airport on November 26, 1974. Delivered to North Central Airlines as N4803C (c/n 39) on March 30, 1962, it was bought by the FAB as TAM 70 on November 26, 1974, the day this picture was taken. It was sold in January 1980 as N511GA to Gulf Air Transport (renamed Gulf Air Inc in March 1986), which sold the aircraft to Air Cape from South Africa as ZS-LYL on April 25, 1988. Air Cape changed its name to Safair in October 1988. It was bought by the Court Helicopter Company in December 1993 and operated with Court Air in November 2010. In September 2017, it was preserved and put on display at the Wijnland Auto Museum, Cape Town, as ZS-LYL in Safair colors.

Frigorifico Reyes Boeing B-17G CP-891 at the airline's ramp at La Paz El Alto Airport on November 26, 1974. CP-891 was one of the last B-17s operated in Bolivia to haul beef from remote ranches in eastern Bolivia to La Paz El Alto Airport, and after its service ended it was bought by the March Field Air Museum in Riverside, California. A Bolivian crew ferried the Boeing B-17G to Nogales Airport in Arizona on December 17, 1980, and on January 10, 1981, it flew to March AFB. In 2017, the B-17G, now carrying the serial 44-6393, was refurbished to show how this aircraft would have appeared in 1945; it was given the name *Starduster* and Mediterranean Allied Air Forces markings were added.

Frigorifico Reyes Boeing B-17's CP-753 and CP-891 at the airline's ramp at La Paz El Alto Airport on November 26, 1974. Both B-17s survive at Riverside and Paine Field museums in the US.

FRIMO Curtiss C-46D CP-777 at La Paz El Alto Airport on November 21, 1973, having various goods unloaded, including a lot of fresh meat. The aircraft had arrived from a big hazienda near Trinidad in the north of Bolivia, carrying three tons of fresh meat. The climate in the north is tropical, and in-flight temperature control is not available, therefore merchandise has to arrive at the market in La Paz as soon as possible. La Paz is the highest capital in the world, sitting at 3,600m in a natural basin. It has 800,000 inhabitants, and the immediate surroundings offer no hope for any worthwhile agricultural production. In the Beni Department of Bolivia, meat can be purchased for US$0.25 per lb, but in La Paz the price is four times higher.

CP-777 FRIMO Cutiss C-46D during some maintenance at La Paz El Alto Airport on November 26, 1974. La Paz El Alto Airport, which sits at 4,061.5m (13,325ft) is one of the highest airports in the world. As a result, the air is thinner, and therefore aircraft require longer runways to accumulate the amount of lift needed for take-off; as a result, runway 10R/28L measures 4,000m (13,123ft) in length to enable larger, heavier aircraft to operate. The spectacular natural backdrop features the snow-covered Mount Illimani, the second highest peak in Bolivia at 6,438m (21,122ft).

TURMO Douglas C-54G CP-1090 at Cochabamba Airport on November 20, 1974. Delivered to the USAAF as 45-0583 with c/n 36036 on August 28, 1945, it transferred to the United States Coast Guard in 1958 as 45-0583 and converted to EC-54U standard. It was sold to the Charlotte Aircraft Corporation in October 1967 as N17225, then leased to Polynesian Airlines on March 14, 1968 as 5W-FAD. The aircraft was repossessed on August 20, 1969, as N6299, and then leased to Ecuatoriana as HC-ASC in 1970. It returned to the Charlotte Aircraft Corporation in 1972, after which it was bought by TURMO in May 1974 as CP-1090, wfu and stored at Cochabamba Airport in 1977, then sold to North East Bolivian Airways in 1979. After take-off from Cochabamba Airport on January 13, 1984, the number two engine failed; the crew was cleared to return for an emergency landing, but the C-54G was unstable on the final approach and the pilot lost control, veered off the runway to the left and came to rest in a drainage ditch. One crew member was killed, two others were injured, and the Douglas C-54G was damaged beyond repair.

Centro de Entrenamiento Aeronautico Douglas C-47A CP-583 at Cochabamba Airport on November 20, 1974. Delivered to the USAAF as 42-23806 (c/n 9668) in June 1943, it was transferred to the Royal Flying Corps on November 16, 1945, and was then bought by V. V. Vasconcelos as PP-XAZ in 1946. It was bought as PP-LPE in November 1946 by Linhas Aereas Paulistas, which merged with Loide Aereo Nacional in April 1951. The aircraft was then bought by LAB as CB-83 on July 22, 1951, and reregistered as CP-583 in October 1953. Next it was leased to CEAC and VIBAS in 1974, then Lineas Aereas Canedo in August 1979, before being sold to Transportes Aereos Alfa by 1982 and seized in 1990 for drug trafficking at Trinidad Airport in Bolivia. It was wfu and stored, still at Trinidad Airport, in 2015.

Chacaltaya is located in the Cordillera Real mountain range in western Bolivia and reaches 5,421m (17,785ft). From the top of Chacaltaya, you have a fantastic view of La Paz city and La Paz El Alto airport, as well as the numerous peaks in the surrounding area.

Chapter 9

Peru

Faucett Compania de Aviacion, S.A. Douglas C-47A OB-R-544 departs Cuzco Airport on December 4, 1973. Delivered to the USAAF as 42-93283 (c/n 13177) in 1942, it was bought by Wheeler Airlines as CF-DME, and then crashed near Arctic Bay Airport in Canada on May 14, 1958, when it collided with a snow-covered mountain top; there were no fatalities and the aircraft was repaired. Faucett purchased it as OB-PBJ, later reregistering it as OB-R-544, and it was next bought by the Peruvian Navy (Marina de Guerra del Perú) as AT-521. It was sold to Hel Peruano as OB-1756 in 2001, and then bought by Aerolineas de La Paz as HK-4292. In July 2013, it was seen in storage at Villavicencio Vanguardia Airport.

Peruvian Air Force (Fuerza Aérea del Perú, FAP) Douglas C-54D FAP 386 arriving at Lima Jorge Chávez International Airport on December 5, 1973. Delivered as 42-72499 (c/n 10604) to the USAAF, it was bought by the FAP as FAP 386 on July 27, 1966, and then transferred to Commercial Transport Air Service (Servicio Aereo de Transportes Comerciales, SATCO) as FAP 386 in April 1972. It returned to the FAP in May 1973, and is assumed to have been broken up.

FAP De Havilland Canada DHC.5A Buffalo FAP 323 at Lima Jorge Chávez International Airport on December 5, 1973. Delivered on December 7, 1971 as FAP 323 (c/n 46), it was stored at Jorge Chávez in 1985. Sixteen DHC.5As were delivered between 1971 and 1972 for use by Grupo 41.

Faucett Douglas C-54A OB-R-247 departing from Lima Jorge Chávez International Airport on December 5, 1973. This aircraft was delivered to the USAAF with serial 42-107443 (c/n 7462) on January 21, 1944. Following this, it was bought by the South American Trading Corporation as N42987 in 1946, and sold to Flota Aerea Mercante Argentina as LV-ABM in the same year. On August 4, 1950, it was bought by Faucett as OB-PBB-247 and reregistered as OB-R-247 in 1964. On December 30, 1976, the C-54A departed Trujillo Airport for a flight to Tarapoto Airport; on the take-off climb, the Douglas C-54A struck the slope of Mount Pintado, located 25km north of the airport. The wreckage was found a few hours later in a rocky area; all 24 passengers and crew members were killed, and the aircraft was damaged beyond repair.

Aerotransportes Entre Rios
Curtiss C-46A LV-FTR, having
just arrived at Lima Jorge
Chávez International Airport on
December 5, 1973. Delivered to
the USAAF on April 27, 1944, as
42-61061 (c/n 26936), it was
bought by the Indian government
on April 10, 1946, then ferried back
to Miami Airport as N408K on an
unknown date. In March 1957, it
was bought by Transcontinental as
LV-PCV, and reregistered as LV-FTR
on April 12, 1957. It was leased to
Austral in December 1961, returning
in February 1962, and sold to
Aerotransportes Entre Rios in October
1964. It was wfu at Montevideo
Carrasco Airport during 1974 and
broken up in February 1979.

FAP Douglas C-47A FAP-373
having just arrived at Lima Jorge
Chávez International Airport on
December 5, 1973. It was delivered to
the USAAF as 42-100531 (c/n 18994).
Over 30 C-47As were taken on charge
and operated by SATCO, TANS Perú
and Grupo de Comunicaciones 8.
Six were still in use in 1977, and,
FAP-357, is on display at the Las
Palmas Air Base near Lima.

Peruvian Navy Sud SA.316
Alouette III HAS-420 at Lima Jorge
Chávez International Airport on
December 5, 1973.

Faucett Douglas DC-6B OB-R-846 at Lima Jorge Chávez International Airport on December 8, 1973. Delivered to Japan Air Lines as registration JA6205 *City of Nagoya* (c/n 44432) on September 24, 1954, it was bought by Faucett on August 20, 1966 as OB-R-246, and reregistered as OB-R-846 on September 9, 1966. In 1980, it was wfu and it was broken up in June 1981 at Lima Jorge Chávez. Faucett was founded on September 15, 1928, commencing operations on September 27, 1928, and ceasing on December 3, 1997.

Pesquera Humboldt S.A. Fairchild F-27A OB-M-950 at Lima Jorge Chávez International Airport on December 8, 1973. Delivered to Executive Properties Inc on March 13, 1959, it was leased to the Kimberley-Clark Corporation as N200KC (c/n 41) on the same day. It returned to Executive Properties Inc on March 25, 1971, and was subsequently bought by Pesquera Humboldt S.A. from Peru as OB-M-950. It was converted from F-27A to F-27J (freighter) in 1974 and sold to the Ministry of Fisheries (Ministerio de Pesquería) in 1974. It was bought by ATC Inc in August 1981 as N927, and leased to Pyramid Airlines in June 1982, after which it was bought by Rockwell International Corporation and reregistered as N64NR in February 1985. It was scrapped at an unknown location in October 1987.

Venezuelan Air Force (Fuerza Aérea Venezolana, FAV) Lockheed C-130H 4224 arriving at Lima Jorge Chávez International Airport on November 2, 1977. Delivered to the FAV in February 1975 as FAV 4224 (c/n 4556), it was based at Palo Negro Air Base (Base Aérea Palo Negro) with Transport Squadron No 1 (Escuadron de Transporte No 1).

Aeroperú Fokker F-27-600 OB-R-1082 at Lima Jorge Chávez International Airport on November 2, 1977. Delivered on July 23, 1975, as OB-R-1082 (c/n 10514), it was sold to Air North as N60AN in January 1984. The company merged with Brockway Air on October 1, 1984, and sold the aircraft to First Security Bank of Utah in February 1985, which then leased it back to Brockway Air. It returned to First Bank in December 1987 and was subsequently leased to SAAB Aircraft Holdings Inc in December 1987, then to Mesaba Airlines from January 25, 1988 until November 1994. It was with Southern Cross Aviation Camarillo in California on November 16, 1994, but the N60AN registration was cancelled shortly after on November 22, 1994. It was bought by WDL Aviation on November 20, 1994, as D-AELI, and broken up in February 2009 at Cologne Bonn Airport.

Peruvian Navy (Marina de Guerra del Perú) Fokker F-27-400MAR AE-560 at Lima Jorge Chávez International Airport on November 2, 1977. First flown as PH-EXD on June 14, 1977, it was delivered to the Peruvian Navy on September 17, 1977 as AE-560 (c/n 10548). On December 8, 1987, while flying from Pucallpa Airport to Jorge Chávez, the Fokker crashed at 2015hrs at sea, 11km northwest of Lima. The captain was the only survivor of the accident; the subsequent investigation revealed that he had only recorded 5.3 night-flight hours in the 90 days before the accident, 3.3 hours in the last 60 days, and none in the last 30 days, and the co-pilot had only 90 minutes of night-flight experience in the two months before the crash. During the approach to Lima, the crew noticed an indication that the nose gear would not lock down, so a low flyby was made to let the air traffic control tower check the gear. The gear was determined to be okay, but as they made a second approach in darkness, the Fokker F-27-400MAR impacted the water. There were 42 fatalities.

Above: TANS Perú/FAP de Havilland Canada DHC-6-300 42309 at Pucallpa Yarina dock on the Rio Ucayali river, one of the many tributaries of the great Amazon river, on November 4, 1977. The aircraft was delivered on October 5, 1973, as FAP 309 (c/n 384) and subsequently transferred to TANS. Reregistered as OB-R-1158, it was written off following an accident at an oil camp at Trompetereos on November 28, 1983.

Left: FAP-309 takes off on the Rio Ucayali near Pucallpa for a flight to Iquitos, with a stop at Contamana.

Below: The cabin of a de Havilland Twin Otter, with space for 19 passengers and two pilots.

Above left: An FAP captain at Contamana.

Above right: Lisboa is a very small settlement along the Ucayali river, and many people come to watch the Twin Otter.

Orellana is another stop when traveling the Ucayali river.

Above: Flor de Punga.

Left: Take-off along the Ucayali river.

Requena is another short stop off destination.

Approaching the final destination of Iquitos, the Twin Otter flies over the Amazon river for a water landing. The full journey from Pucallpa to Iquitos is 3hrs 10mins and 329 miles, with six stops along the way.

Chapter 10

Ecuador

Above: Andes Airlines Canadair Cl-44-6/CC-106 HC-AZH at Quito Mariscal Sucre International Airport, Ecuador, on October 30, 1977. Delivered to the RCAF on March 30, 1962, with serial 16666 (c/n 13), it was re-serialled as 15932 on May 1, 1962. Following the RCAF's merger with the Canadian Army and Navy to create the Canadian Armed Forces, the aircraft was re-serialled again, this time as 106932, on May 26, 1970. It was bought by Beaver Enterprises on November 18, 1971, as CF-JSN and wfu at Montréal–Dorval International Airport. It was subsequently sold to Andes Airlines as HC-AZH in May 1974 and wfu at Guayaquil Airport in Ecuador in January 1986. In October 2010, it was moved to the May Day nightclub in Cuenca, Ecuador. The RCAF announced an order for further Canadair CL-44 variants under the designation CC-106. The CL-44 was basically a stretched version of the Bristol Britannia 253, and was intended to be powered by Orion engines, but this was changed to Rolls-Royce Tyne engines before the design was finalized.

Opposite above: SAETA Vickers Viscount V.785D HC-AVP at Quito Mariscal Sucre International Airport on October 28, 1977. The aircraft was delivered to Linea Aeree Italiana on June 30, 1957 as I-LARK (c/n 329), and the company merged with Alitalia on October 1, 1957. It was bought by Andes Líneas Aérea but was not taken up, instead being purchased by SAETA as HC-AVP in August 1971. On the morning of April 23, 1979, the Viscount departed Mariscal Sucre on a scheduled service to Mariscal Lamar International Airport, Cuenca; while cruising at an altitude of 18,000ft, the Viscount struck the slope of a mountain and disappeared from the radar. SAR operations were initiated but eventually abandoned a few days later as no trace was found of the Viscount or the 57 occupants. The wreckage was located about five years later in a mountainous area located in the region of Shell-Mera in the province of Pastaza.

Opposite below: Ecuavia Fairchild FH-227E HC-AYM at Quito Mariscal Sucre International Airport on October 28, 1977. Delivered to Mohawk Airlines as N7805M *City of Glen Falls* (c/n 511) on August 30, 1966, it was sold to the Fairchild-Hiller Corporation on October 26, 1967, and converted to FH-227C standard. It was bought by the Texaco Petroleum Company on October 2, 1972 as HC-AYM, and leased to Ecuavia in October 1972. In December 1993, it was reregistered to Petroecuador, then sold to AerGal in 2000, but operated by Petroecuador. On January 17, 2002, FH-227C was performing a charter flight on behalf of Texaco from Quito Mariscal Sucre to Lago Agrio Airport, Nueva Loja, with 21 oil workers and five crew members on board. During its descent in foggy conditions, the aircraft struck the slope of Mount El Tigre in Columbia, near the border with Ecuador. The wreckage was found three days later at an altitude of 4,500m; all passengers and crew were killed.

Ecuadorian Military Air Transport (Transportes Aéreos Militares Ecuatorianos, TAME) Ecuador Lockheed L-188A HC-AZT arriving from Quito Mariscal Sucre at Guayaquil Airport October 28, 1977. Delivered to Braniff Airways on April 29, 1959, as N9701C (c/n 1040), it was bought by Crocker Citizens National Bank on March 28, 1968, and leased to Braniff Airways on the same day. It returned on March 27, 1969, and was sold to F.B Ayer & Associates on May 26, 1970, where it was wfu and stored at Tucson Airport. It was bought by TAME on February 27, 1975 as HC-AZT with the name *Azuay*. TAME is a branch of the Ecuadorian Air Force (Fuerza Aérea Ecuatoriana, FAE), set up in 1962 to provide domestic passenger and cargo services and to fly supplemental routes within Ecuador that commercial airlines found uneconomical. The aircraft was sold to Varig in April 1968 as PP-VNK, then bought by Filair on November 1, 1993 as 9Q-CDU and stored at Calgary Airport. Air Spray purchased it in March 1994 as C-GBKT, reregistered it as C-GFQA in November 1999. It crashed on July 16, 2003, near Cranbrook, British Columbia, whilst firefighting after the pilots flew into a ridge; both crew members lost their lives.

FAE Hawker Siddeley HS 748-2A HC-AUD/FAE-682 at Guayaquil Airport, October 28, 1977. First flown on September 2, 1970, it was delivered on October 3, 1970, as HC-AUD/FAE-682 (c/n 1682) directly to the FAE. In August 2006, it was seen wfu and stored at Quito Mariscal Sucre International Airport.

ANDES Airlines Ecuador Douglas DC-6A HC-AQB at Guayaquil Airport on October 28, 1977. Delivered to United Airlines as N37594 *Cargoliner Newark* (c/n 44909) on July 13, 1956, it was wfu and stored at San Francisco International Airport in February 1968. California Airmotive purchased the aircraft on November 14, 1968, and it was sold to ANDES Airlines Ecuador in 1969 as HC-AQB. It was wfu and stored at Guayaquil Airport in 1980 and later broken up.

Dragon Ecuatoriana Douglas B-23 HC-APV at Mariscal Quito Sucre International Airport on October 29, 1977. Delivered to the United States Army Air Corps (USAAC) as 39-0031 (c/n 2717) it was bought by Pan American World Airways as NC51436 in 1946, and reregistered as N400W in 1954. Operated for a time as an executive transport by Juan Trippe, it reregistered as N4000W in 1959, then sold to the Carolina Aircraft Corporation, Miami, on August 29, 1968. It was bought by Cia Ecuatoriana de Aviacion in December 1968 as HC-APV, wfu and stored at Mariscal Sucre in 1975, then transferred to the Museo Aeronáutico y Del Espacio De La Fae in 1988.

Americana Douglas C-54G HC-ATL at Quito Mariscal Sucre International Airport on October 29, 1977. It was delivered to the USAAF on July 21, 1945, as 45-0540 (c/n 35993). When the USAAF became the USAF, on September 18, 1947, the aircraft was converted to RC-54V standard and transferred to the United States Coast Guard as 45540 in 1958. It was bought by Bellomy Aviation on August 18, 1964 as N4648S, sold to SAM Colombia as HK-767 in 1968, then bought by Americana in October 1970 as HC-ATL.

FAE Douglas DC-6B HC-AVH/FAE 44691, at the Museo Aeronáutico y Del Espacio De La Fae on October 28, 1977. Delivered to Lan Chile as CC-CLDB (c/n 44691) on February 17, 1955, it was reregistered as CC-CCE in 1956, and bought by TAME/FAE as HC-AVH/FAE 44691 in 1971. It was wfu and stored at Quito Mariscal Sucre International Airport in 1975 before being transferred to the museum in 1976.

FAE de Havilland Canada DHC-6-300 Twin Otter FAE 457 at Quito Mariscal Sucre International Airport on October 30, 1977. This aircraft was from Downsview Airport, Ontario, for the Fuerza Aerea Ecuatoriana on April 24, 1975 as FAE 457 (c/n 457). On July 27, 1979, it overran the runway on take-off from Putumayo and was transported to the Miami Aviation Corporation for repairs. It returned by November 1980 and reregistered as HC-BAX, still with the FAE. On May 22, 1981, on a flight from Mariscal Sucre to José María Velasco Ibarra Airport, Macará, the Twin Otter was destroyed when it crashed into the side of a mountain near Zumba, Ecuador; three crew members and 15 passengers lost their lives.

Chapter 11

Colombia

Aeropesca Vickers Viscount V.745D HK-1708 at Bogotá El Dorado Airport on October 24, 1977. It was delivered to Capital Airlines on September 24, 1956, as N7440 (c/n 138), and, after the company merged with United Air Lines on June 1, 1961, the aircraft was sold to the Viscount International Corporation on January 11, 1969 and stored at Delaware Coastal Airport in Georgetown, Delaware. It was sold to SAETA as N7440 on May 24, 1974, but never operated. It was then bought by Aeropesca on June 30, 1974, as HK-1708 and Intercontinental de Aviacion on June 3, 1983. On March 31, 1991, during a flight from Bogotá El Dorado Airport to Medellin Airport, the Vickers Viscount made an emergency landing at Medellin after two ailerons failed in turbulence; it was damaged beyond repair. It is preserved in a park in the city of Rionegro in the Department of Antioquia, Colombia.

Servicios Especiales Aereos (SEA) Fairchild C-82A Packet HK-426 at Bogotá El Dorado Airport, October 23, 1977. Its name, *Arauca,* which is visible on the nose, is the name of a city in the northeast of Colombia, close to the border of Venezuela. It was delivered to the USAAF as 45-57829 (c/n 10199) in 1945 and was subsequently bought by Ben Widtfeldt and Harry S. McCandless on August 23, 1955, and registered as N6235C. It was bought by LEBCA International on August 31, 1955, then sold to Lace Ltda from Colombia as HK-426 on September 26, 1956. Next, Lilia Lizcano de Herrera from Colombia purchased the aircraft on October 6, 1967, selling it to SEA in 1972. With the latter, it was wfu and stored at Bogotá Airport during 1973. According to the author, "During my last visit to Bogotá El Dorado Airport in February 1993, I did not see the Fairchild C-82A. It had either been removed completely, or moved to the military side of the airport."

Transportes Aereos Tropicales (TAT) Douglas DC-4-1009 HK-173 at Bogotá El Dorado Airport on October 23, 1977. This aircraft was delivered to Svensk interkontinental Lufttrafik AB as SE-BBA (c/n 42905) on May 1, 1946. The company merged with Scandinavian Airlines System (SAS) on August 1, 1948, and SE-BBA was sold to Avianca on September 9, 1953 as HK-173. It was bought by TAT in 1974, wfu and stored at El Dorado without engines in 1976. It was broken up in 2000.

Avianca Hawker Siddeley HS 748-245 HK-1409 at Bogotá El Dorado Airport on October 25, 1977. Delivered to Avianca as HK-1409 (c/n 1658) on October 25, 1968, it was wfu and stored at Bogotá El Dorado Airport in October 1977. Next it was bought by Dan-Air on March 23, 1978 as G-BFLL, and leased to British Airways on April 17, 1982, returning to Dan-Air on January 30, 1985. It was leased again to British Airways on September 4, 1985, until September 30, 1985, and again from November 1, 1986, until April 1, 1987. It was also leased to Aberdeen Airways on March 2, 1990, then bought by Air Provence International in June 1995 as F-GODD. It later transferred to Virgin Express, but operated for Best Air, and was reregistered as S2-ABE. In October 2006, while flying from Wunrok Airstrip Alek Airstrip, both in South Sudan, this aircraft was damaged beyond repair while landing.

Aeropesca Vickers Viscount V.745D HK-1708 at Bogotá Airport on October 26, 1977. Aeropesca formed in 1965, performing scheduled passenger and cargo services with Curtiss C-46 Commandos and Vickers Viscounts. The company ceased operations on June 3, 1983.

Lineas Aereas Del Caribe Douglas (LAC) Douglas C-118A HK-1705 arriving at Leticia Airport on November 8, 1977. Leticia is a municipality and small Colombian city at the border triangle of Colombia, Peru and Brazil. Delivered to the USAF on July 16, 1952 as 51-3818, (c/n 43565), it was stored at Davis Monthan AFB in January 1975, and bought by Desert Air Parts Inc on May 12, 1976. It was sold to LAC in August 1977 as HK-1705; however, on April 29, 1978, it was flying from Bogotá El Dorado Airport to Soledad Airport (now Ernesto Cortissoz International Airport) when the aircraft struck a tree, broke up and was damaged beyond repair; all three crew members and five of the nine passengers on board were killed.

Aerosucre Colombia S.A. Douglas DC-6A/B HK-1701 at Leticia Airport on November 8, 1977. Delivered to SABENA as OO-SDG (c/n 43828) on April 1, 1953, it was leased to Aviaco in both 1962 and 1963 as EC-ASR, returning to SABENA in November 1963. It was bought by the Luftwaffe as CA+023 in May 1965 and converted to a Douglas DC-6B, after which it was reregistered as 13+01 in 1967. Sold to Sterling Airways as OY-STZ on June 5, 1969, it was then leased to Trollair in March 1972, returning to Sterling Airways in June 1972. Oriental Pearl Airways purchased the aircraft as VR-HGW on September 23, 1972, and then sold it soon after to the Charlotte Aircraft Corporation in July 1973 as N90535. It was sold to Cessnyca Colombia in March 1975 as HK-1701X and bought by Aerosucre Colombia as HK-1701 in October 1976. On November 8, 1977, the nose gear collapsed at Leticia Airport, but there was never any official report about the accident.

Aeropesca Colombia Curtiss C-46A HK-388 at Leticia Airport on November 8, 1977. Delivered to the USAAF on February 9, 1944, as 43-3663 (c/n 26796), it was transferred to the Reconstruction Finance Corporation on November 25, 1945, then wfu and stored at Ontario Airport in the same month. It was sold to Neil F. Lawrence in 1948 as N79979, leased to Contreras Manual as XA-HIO in 1949, and returned in November 1949. The Allied Aircraft Company purchased the aircraft in March 1951, and sold it to Aerovias Brasil as PP-AXU on June 28, 1951. It was bought by San Venezuela as YV-C-NAF in March 1954, sold to LIDCA Colombia as HK-388 in October 1954, and then bought by Aeropesca Colombia on June 23, 1965.

Right: Aeropesca Colombia Curtiss C-46A HK-388 at Leticia Airport. The author recalls: "This is where we boarded our flight to Bogotá. We only paid $40 US dollars between us for this flight, and the journey itself was four hours long."

Below: A view from Curtiss C-46A HK-388's cockpit.

"On the journey from Leticia to Bogotá, the cargo was mainly fresh fish from the Amazon river, but there was also a lot of dried fish that was packed in jute bags. The smell was terrible, but luckily there were a few holes in the fuselage for fresh air."

Left: C-46A HK-388 had two Pratt & Whitney R-2800s engines of 2,000hp each. Maximum speed: 245mph Cruising speed: 175mph: Range 1,200 miles.

Below: A view from the cockpit shortly before arriving at Bogotá El Dorado Airport.

On October 21, 1981, HK-388 was hijacked on a flight from Medellin to Barranquilla. The hijackers demanded that the crew land at the Guajira Peninsula, where they loaded five tons of weapons, then departed again before forcing another landing in the Rio Orteguaza river. There, weapons were unloaded, the aircraft was abandoned, and the C-46A was damaged beyond repair.

Douglas C-47 FAC 658 at Medellin Airport on November 13, 1980.

Aerolineas Medellin Douglas DC-4A HK-528 at Medellin Airport on November 13, 1980. Delivered to the USAAF as Douglas C-54B 42-72344 (c/n 10449) on November 27, 1944, this aircraft was converted to a Douglas DC-4A on January 5, 1946. It was bought by Pan American World Airways as N88902 on July 17, 1946, then Eastern Air Lines on November 7, 1950, and Aero Leases in May 1955. While with Aero Leases, it returned to Eastern Air Lines under lease until 1960, after which it was bought by the Trans Equipment Company on May 20, 1960. SAM Colombia purchased it in 1968 as HK-528, then sold it to Aerotabo Colombia in 1974, which was rebranded as Aerolineas Medellin in 1976. It was wfu at Medellin Airport in 1978 and broken up by 1988; the fuselage was still at the airport without engines and undercarriage in November 1992.

SATENA Douglas C-54G FAC-1105 at Bogotá El Dorado Airport on November 15, 1980. It was delivered to the USAAF as 45-0571 (c/n 36024) on August 13, 1945, then leased to Pan American World Airways as N88943 in 1946. In 1949, it was leased to United Air Lines, and then Flying Tiger Line in 1951. It returned to the USAF in 1954, with the registration 45-0571. SATENA purchased it as FAC 697, then reregistered it as FAC-1105 in 1976. In April 1983, it was known to be derelict at El Dorado, and has since been broken up.

SATENA Douglas C-54G FAC 1105. SATENA is a military airline that came into being in September 1962 with a mix of Consolidated PBY Catalinas and de Havilland Beavers. Following reorganization in 1966, SATENA flew a mixture of Douglas C-47s and, C-54s and Hawker Siddeley HS-748s. The airline links Bogotá with the country's main population centres as well as distant jungle airstrips.

A SATENA Douglas C-54G FAC 1105 flight from Bogotá to Villavicencio. The interior is basic, but it could accommodate 56 passengers along with five crew members.

Right: FAC 1105 was powered by two Pratt & Whitney R-2000-9 Twin Wasp 14-cylinder air-cooled radial piston engines.

Below: FAC 1105 arrives at Villavicencio Vanguardia Airport after a 30 min flight from Bogotá.

FAC 1105 is soon to depart from Villavicencio Vanguardia Airport towards Bogotá El Dorado Airport.

Left: **Flying over Bogotá just before sunset.**

Below: **Aeropesca Colombia Curtiss C-46 Commando HK-388 at Villavicencio Vanguardia Airport on November 15, 1980.**

ARCA Colombia Douglas C-47A HK-339 at Villavicencio Vanguardia Airport, stored without engines, on November 15, 1980. This aircraft was delivered to the USAAF as 42-92218 (c/n 11994) on October 23, 1943, and as part of the US–UK lend-lease program, the Royal Air Force's (RAF) 512 Sqn acquired it on December 1, 1943, as FL586. It was returned to the USAF on December 4, 1946. In the same month, it was sold to KLM West Indies as PJ-ALH, then bought by SAM Colombia as HK-522 in December 1951 but not taken up, so it was registered to ARCA Colombia as HK-339 in December 1954. By 1977, it was wfu at Vanguardia.

El Venado Colombia Douglas C-54G HK2017 at Villavicencio Vanguardia Airport on November 15, 1980. Delivered to the USAAF as 45-0521 (c/n 35974) on July 13, 1945, it was wfu and stored at Davis Monthan AFB in September 1972. It was bought by Dross Metals Inc on November 13, 1975, as N3370F; sold to Aircraft & Export Inc on September 15, 1976; bought by TANA Colombia on March 2, 1977, as HK-2017; sold to Taxi Aereo El Venado in 1978; bought by ATA Colombia in 1981; then sold to Aerolineas del Este in 1986. AVESCA purchased the aircraft in 1988, but later withdrew it and stored it at Vanguardia. It was sold to Transapel in December 1997, then once again stored at Villavicencio Vanguardia Airport, this time on May 12, 2000. It was broken up in January 2001.

Transamazonica Colombia Douglas C-47-DL HK-1315 at Villavicencio Vanguardia Airport on November 15, 1980. It was delivered to the USAAF as 41-7808 (c/n 4307) on April 24, 1942, and was wfu by November 1945. It was bought by Lone Star Air Cargo as NC50037 in September 1946. Between 1946 and its time with Transamazonica, it operated with Transportes Aereos Nacional, REAL and Varig as PP-AN; then Avianca, Lineas Aereas La Urraca and Taxi Aereo El Venado as HK-1315. It was purchased by Transamazonica in November 1980, sold to TAERCO, VIARCO, SADELCA and finally Allas Colombia, in 2014. On July 21, 2022, whilst flying from Trujillo Airport to Barranco Minas Airport, the C-47-DL suffered a burst main tire upon landing; the tail gear collapsed and the aircraft veered off the runway, but there were no fatalities.

Aerolineas del Este (ADES) Beech D-18S HK-1214 at Villavicencio Vanguardia Airport on November 15, 1980. Delivered to Anderson Air Activities as N8936A (c/n A-584) on February 8, 1957, it was sold to Chelsea Holdings in 1957 as CF-JNQ, then bought by Louis Cadesky Associates in 1965. It was sold to Glen Lake Silver Mines in 1970 and bought by Jamie M. Castro as HK-1215P on March 24, 1971. It was reregistered as HK-1214 on November 11, 1973, for Aerolineas del Este, and was seen derelict at Medellin Airport by 1985.

Transamazonica Colombia Douglas DC-3A HK-1340 at Villavicencio Vanguardia Airport on November 15, 1980. Delivered to the USAAF as a Douglas C-53D 42-68777 (c/n 11704) on May 12, 1943, it was leased to Pan American World Airways as NC19118 in April 1945, then bought by the airline in 1949 and converted to a Douglas DC-3A. It was wfu in December 1966, but quickly sold in the same month to Avianca Colombia as HK-1340. Taxi Aereo del Venado purchased the aircraft in October 1973, after which it was transferred to Transamazonica and then sold to LACOL Colombia. On July 7, 1985, the DC-3A was flying from Villavicencio to Caruru when shortly after take-off the right engine caught fire; the aircraft lost height, struck trees and crashed a few kilometers from the airport, bursting into flames. Subsequent investigation showed that the right engine failed because the total weight of the DC-3A was well above the maximum take-off weight; there were three fatalities and three survivors.

SATENA Douglas C-53-D FAC 1128 at Bogotá El Dorado Airport on November 17, 1980. The USAAF received the aircraft as 41-20054 (c/n 4824) on October 30, 1941, and loaned it to the RAAF as VH-CCC on November 5, 1941. It returned to the USAAF on April 27, 1944, and was sold to Philippine Air Lines as PI-C150 in September 1948. Next it was bought by a private owner as N73421 on September 22, 1952; it then sold to the FAC as FAC 670, transferring to SATENA as FAC 1128. On August 3, 1981, the C-53-D was engaged in a local post-maintenance test flight at Palmaseca International Airport (later Alfonso Bonilla Aragón Airport), when, during the climb, one of the engines failed and the captain attempted an emergency landing. The C-53-D crashed on a farm near the airport, and while all four crew were injured, there were no fatalities.

An early morning line-up of four Douglas DC-3s and a Curtis C-46A Commando of Selva Columbia, at Villavicencio Vanguardia Airport on November 9, 1983.

Selva Colombia Curtiss C-46A HK-851 at Villavicencio Vanguardia Airport on November 9, 1983. Delivered to the USAAF on May 18, 1945, as 43-47311 (c/n 2926), it was bought by the Indian government on April 10, 1946, then sold to a private owner and ferried via Prestwick in Scotland to Panama as HP-217 on September 17, 1955. It was bought by LIDCA Colombia as HK-851 on June 5, 1956; Aerocondor in November 1957; Aeronorte S.A. in 1976; Selva in May 1982; Aeronorte S.A. again in December 1983; Selva again in 1985; Coral Colombia in 1989; and finally by Rolando Medina Marmolejo on May 1, 2000, as HK-851. On July 9, 2000, the aircraft was prepared for a flight from Villavicencio Vanguardia Airport to Mitú Airport, but shortly after take-off the right-hand engine caught fire. The pilot attempted to return to the airport by executing a sharp right-hand turn but lost control and the C-46A crashed. Subsequent investigation showed that, while the aircraft was certified to carry a maximum of 13 occupants, the flight plan indicated that the flight had two pilots and 17 passengers. Moreover, it was revealed that the aircraft was not in an airworthy condition, the flight experience of the two pilots had not been logged, and the captain and owner of the C-46A did not have a valid medical certificate. There were 19 fatalities.

Lineas Aereas El Dorado Ltda Douglas C-47A HK-2666 at Villavicencio Vanguardia Airport on November 9, 1983. Delivered to the USAAF as 42-24339 (c/n 10201) on September 8, 1943, it transferred to the RCAF with the serial 662 on September 16, 1943. It was sold to the Omani Air Force with the serial 502 on June 30, 1969, then bought by Bergen Air Transport as LN-TVA on September 16, 1972. Ontario Central Airlines purchased the aircraft as C-GSTA on December 22, 1980, then sold it to Lineas Aereas El Dorado Ltda in 1987 as HK-2666. Next it went to LAS Cargo in February 1992 as HK-2666-P, then ADES in 1998 and Aeroejecutivos S.A. on July 21, 2006, this time as YV-211T. It was wfu and stored at Caracas Maiquetía Airport in 2008.

SATENA Pilatus PC-6/B2-H2 Turbo Porter FAC 1113 *El Piapoco* at Villavicencio Vanguardia Airport on November 9, 1983. This aircraft was delivered to SATENA from the Pilatus factory in Switzerland as HB-FHT (c/n 822) on 12 August 1983 and was reregistered as FAC 1113. The PC-6 was mainly used to fly to remote airstrips in the jungle of Colombia, and was written off and damaged beyond repair at an unknown location in February 1987; little information is available about the crash, but a few months later, on June 25, 1987, SATENA lost a second PC-6, FAC-1114, near Guapi in the province of Cauca, when it was damaged beyond repair.

FAC Douglas DC-4-1009 FAC-690 arriving at Medellin Airport on November 11, 1983. On May 10, 1946, SE-BBC *Passad* (c/n 42926) was delivered to Swedish Intercontinental Airlines (SILA), which merged with Scandinavian Airline System (SAS) on August 1, 1948; the aircraft was reregistered as OY-DFY *Sigvard Viking* on July 17, 1950. The FAC purchased the aircraft on March 6, 1954, as FAC-690; it was wfu in 1984 at Bogotá El Dorado Airport, and preserved at the Museo Aeroespacial Fuerza Aérea Colombiana at Bogotá El Dorado Airport in 1994.

SATENA Hawker Siddeley HS 748-2A FAC-1102 at Medellin Airport on November 11, 1983. Hawker Siddeley Aviation first flew this aircraft on August 25, 1971, as G-11-2 (c/n 1703). On March 3, 1972, it was sold to SATENA as FAC-1102. On February 25, 1985, the right engine failed 20 minutes after take-off at Bogotá El Dorado Airport; the pilot tried to return to the runway, but during the approach the left engine failed, and the HS 748-2A made a belly landing. There were no fatalities, and the aircraft was repaired. After being purchased by West Air Sweden in 1997 and flown to Linkoping in Sweden, it was used for parts and scrapped.

Lineas Aereas Suramericanas Colombia Curtiss C-46F HK-3205 at Bogotá El Dorado Airport on February 22, 1993. Maintenance crew are hard at work to solve an engine problem.

Cargo Three Panama Convair CV-440-11 HP-1200CTH at Bogotá El Dorado Airport on February 19, 1993. Delivered to Swissair as HB-IMM *Zug* (c/n 413) on April 3, 1957, it was wfu and stored in November 1968. It was then bought by Pan Adria as YU-ADS on November 25, 1969. By 1975, it was wfu once again and stored at Zagreb Airport in Yugoslavia, and by 1976 it had been sold to Associated Products of America as N47099. It was bought by the Florida Aircraft Leasing Corporation (FALC) in August 1979 and leased to Dow Jones in 1981, returning to FALC in 1983; it was then sold to C&M Airways on March 21, 1985 and bought by Cargo Three Panama as HP-1200CTH in September 1991. On February 20, 1993, during take-off from Bogotá El Dorado Airport, the aircraft suffered engine failure and was cleared to return to the airport when it crashed into a nearby field; the two crew members died.

Trans Oriente Colombia Douglas C-47A (R4D-5) HK-3220 arriving at Villavicencio Vanguardia Airport on February 20, 1993. Delivered to the USAAF as a Douglas C-47A with the serial 42-108796 (c/n 11808), it was later designated as a Douglas R4D-5 with serial 17094. Over the next few years, it was in service with several private owners and operators and registrations N7232C, N39, N39AH, and N239GB, and was probably delivered to Trans Oriente in 1989 as HK-3220. On August 31, 1993, on a flight from Sub Teniente Nestor Arias Airport, San Felipe, on the border of Venezuela, to Vanguardia, with a cargo of straw, one of the engines failed; the crew decided to divert to Barranco Minas Airport, but during the approach the R4D-5 failed to stop on the runway and overran into the Rio Guaviare river. The captain and three passengers were rescued, but two other crew members went missing, and the aircraft was damaged beyond repair.

Coral Coronado Aerolineas Curtiss C-46A Commando HK-851 about to depart for Mitú Airport on February 20, 1993. Unfortunately, on July 9, 2000, the aircraft crashed during take-off at Villavicencio Vanguardia Airport when it exceeded the maximum weight capacity.

Tagua Colombia Douglas C-47A HK-3349 arriving at Villavicencio Vanguardia Airport on February 20, 1993. Delivered to the USAAF in June 1943 as 42-92066 with (c/n 11825), it was bought by the FAE as FAE 92066 in January 1948; it then transferred to TAME in 1971 as HC-AVC. It was sold to SAEP as HK-3349 in 1991, and was then bought by Taxi Aereo del Guaviare (TAGUA) as HK-3349X in January 1993. It sold to Aerovilla in November 1993 as HK-3349. Next, it transferred to VIARCO in September 1995, was wfu at Vanguardia, and then moved to Tiuma Theme Park southwest of Villavicencio and placed on top of a tall steel tower.

ALIANSA Douglas C-47A HK-2820 at Villavicencio Vanguardia Airport on February 20, 1993. This aircraft was delivered to the USAAF as 43-15705 (c/n 20171), was bought by Northwest Orient Airlines as NC-79055 in November 1951, and then sold to Ozark Air Lines as N151D in October 1958. The registration was cancelled in 1974, and the aircraft was impounded at Bogotá El Dorado Airport in 1976 as HK-2820X. It was bought by Aliansa in 1982 as HK-2820 and was still active as recently as 2015; however, on July 8, 2021, it crashed during a training flight from Villavicencio Vanguardia Airport due to low visibility and rain in a mountainous area 13.5km from the airport.

Aires Colombia Fairchild F-27J HK-3735X at Bogotá El Dorado Airport on February 21, 1993. Delivered to the Reynolds Metal Company on December 1, 1959, as N991 (c/n 68), it has a long list of operators and lease companies, including: Alton Box Board, Boomtown Casino, Swedair, Aces Colombia, Aires Colombia, Aerocar Colombia and Aero Continente Peru. It was delivered to Aero Continente Peru as OB-1589 in November 1994, and was wfu and stored at Opa-Locka Airport by 2004.

Líneas Aéreas Suramericanas Douglas DC-6A HK-3644X at Bogotá El Dorado Airport, February 22, 1993. Delivered to the United States Navy on May 1, 1953 as 131611 (c/n 43714), it was wfu and stored at Davis Monthan AFB in June 1977. It was bought by Desert Eagle Aviation in September 1989 as N821CS, and then sold to Florida Aircraft Leasing in February 1991. It was subsequently leased to Líneas Aéreas Suramericanas in July 1991 as HK-3644X, returned in May 1994, then leased to Aeronorte Colombia until May 1998. Another lease was to Transportes Aéreos del Pacifico in May 1998, after which it was stored at Bucaramanga Airport, in the province of Santander. It is now preserved along the main road between Bogotá and Bucaramanga.

Líneas Aéreas Suramericanas Curtiss C-46A HK-1856 at Bogotá El Dorado Airport on February 22, 1993. This aircraft was delivered to the USAAF as 43-47298 (c/n 369) on April 20, 1945, and as part of the lend-lease with China, it was leased to the China National Aviation Corporation on April 29, 1945. It was reregistered as N8365C on December 19, 1949, and was subsequently operated by a considerable number of airlines, including Civil Air Transport, World Wide Airways, Bellomy Lawson Aviation, C.L.T.M Airlines, LAU Lineas Aereas La Urraca, and Aeronorte Aerovias del Norte S.A. in 1980 as HK-1856, the last of which rebranded as Líneas Aéreas Suramericanas in 1986. Finally, it was bought by Transoceanica de Aviacion in December 1993. On January 30, 1994, while flying from Bogotá El Dorado Airport to Puerto Inrida, near the border of Venezuela, the C-46A crashed when the wheels sank into the unpaved runway surface, which was soft following heavy rain fall, causing the undercarriage to collapse. The aircraft was damaged beyond repair, but there were no fatalities.

RANSA Colombia Douglas C-54A HK-1028 at Bogotá El Dorado Airport on February 21, 1993. Delivered to the USAAF as 41-37281 (c/n 3071) on March 31, 1943, this aircraft was sold to American Airlines as N90407 in 1946, then bought by US Overseas Airlines on May 25, 1953. It was leased to Flying Tiger Line, Transocean Air Lines and Overseas Colonial Airways, returning to US Overseas Airlines on December 20, 1957. The Air Carrier Service Corporation purchased the aircraft on July 3, 1964, but then sold it to Taxader Colombia as HK-1028 in 1964. Next it was sold to Aerotaxi Colombia in 1967, and then transferred to SAM Colombia in 1970; it was bought by Aerotabo Colombia in 1975 as HK-1028E, and then sold to Lineas Aereas Suramericanas in 1987. It was bought by ALVEA Ltda as HK-1028W, wfu and stored at Bogotá El Dorado Airport, and then sold to RANSA Colombia in 1992. It was later stored again, this time as HK-1028, in February 1997. It was scrapped during 2013.

Líneas Aéreas Suramericanas Curtiss C-46F HK-3205 departing Villavicencio Vanguardia Airport on February 19, 1993. It was delivered to the USAAF as 44-78578 (c/n 22401) in July 1945, and leased to Trans Caribbean Airways on June 4, 1948, returning to the (by this time) USAF in 1954. It was bought by Trans Caribbean Airways as N69346, and was subsequently operated by a considerable number of airlines, including: Meteor Air Transport, Capitol Airways, Air America, Aerovias Nacionales, Ancar Aviation, Inter-Air Inc, and Golden Airways. Aeronorte Colombia bought the C-46F on October 16, 1984, and sold it to Transoceania de Aviacon on March 11, 1994. It was seen with Transamazonica titles as HK-3205P in February 1995, before being bought by Nicky Scherrer in October of that year.

Other books you might like:

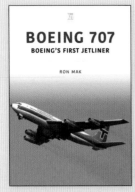

Historic Commercial Aircraft Series, Vol. 2

Historic Commercial Aircraft Series, Vol. 14

Historic Commercial Aircraft Series, Vol. 7

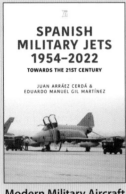

Modern Military Aircraft Series, Vol. 10

Air Forces Series, Vol. 3

Modern Military Aircraft Series, Vol. 9

For our full range of titles please visit:
shop.keypublishing.com/books

VIP Book Club

Sign up today and receive
TWO FREE E-BOOKS

Be the first to find out about our forthcoming
book releases and receive exclusive offers.

Register now at keypublishing.com/vip-book-club

*Our VIP Book Club is a 100% spam-free zone, and we will never share your email with anyone else.
You can read our full privacy policy at: privacy.keypublishing.com*